THE WEATHERING

For Karel at Carol
with happy memories of our
reunion — on the cusp of Fall,
2014 —

R.

ALSO BY RENNIE McQUILKIN

THE WEATHERING

New & Selected Poems

1969 – 2009

Rennie McQuilkin

Antrim House

Simsbury, Connecticut

Library of Congress Cataloging-in-Publication Data

McQuilkin, Rennie, 1936-
The weathering : new & selected poems / by Rennie McQuilkin. – 1st ed.
p. cm.
ISBN 978-0-9798451-7-8 (alk. paper)
I. Title.
PS3563.C65W43 2008
811'.54–dc22
2008035119

Printed & bound by United Graphics. Inc.

First edition, 2009

Cover art: "Northern Point" (detail), Andrew Newell Wyeth (1917-)
egg tempera on gesso panel, 36" x 18 ¼" (1950)
from the collection of the Wadsworth Atheneum of Art

Photograph of author: Pit Pinegar

Antrim House
860.217.0023
AntrimHouse@comcast.net
www.AntrimHouseBooks.com
P.O. Box 111, Tariffville, CT 06081

ACKNOWLEDGEMENTS

The following publications first presented poems appearing in this volume, often in earlier versions:

The American Scholar: "After Waterloo, What"

Anthology of Magazine Verse & Yearbook of American Poetry: "And God Bless Harry," "Mark's Auto Parts" (as "Mark's Used Parts"), "Greenhouse" (as "New England Greenhouse"), "Your Things"

The Atlantic Monthly: "Mark's Auto Parts" (as "Mark's Used Parts"), "Regatta," "The Reverend Robert Walker Skates," "Sister Marie Angelica Plays Badminton," "Twelve," "We All Fall Down"

The Autumn House Anthology of Contemporary American Poetry: "Regatta," "Sister Marie Angelica Plays Badminton"

Beloit Poetry Journal: "The Balancing" (as "Balancing"), "Cecropia," "The Darkening," "Home Burial" (as "Burial"), "Killing Time"

Chelsea: "Henri Raymond Marie de Toulouse-Lautrec-Montfa," "Home Birth," "The Testing," "Valentine"

Cincinnati Poetry Review: "Diorama" (as "Between One World and the Other")

College English: "The Pass," "The Zenith"

The Connecticut Review: "The Rector's Wife"

Connecticut River Review: "Thanksgiving, Fin de Siècle"

Contemporary New England Poetry, A Sampler: "In Wyeth," "The Reverend Robert Walker Skates," "Sister Marie Angelica Plays Badminton"

Crazyhorse: "Admission"

Freshwater: "Last," "Morning"

The Gettysburg Review: "End of the Season," "Learning the Angels," "Self-Portraits," "Solstice"

Hiram Poetry Review: "Swamp Song"

The Hudson Review: "The Lighters," "Riding the Tire"

Joyful Noise: An Anthology of American Spiritual Poetry: "Small Life Rising" (as "Ascension")

The Kansas Quarterly: "Black Ice"

The Literary Review: "Desert," "Invitation," "Lines," "So Much Mourning," "Training the Eyes"

The Malahat Review: "Flower Farmer," "It's Been a Long Long Time," "Locksmith," "The Mugging," "The Son"

Margie: The American Journal of Poetry: "On Assignment in Uganda"

Nimrod: "The Hole" (as "In the Canyon")

The North American Review: "War News"

Northeast: "Wildflowers," "Skunk Cabbage"

Ontario Review: "Break Up," "The Collecting," "The Naming"

Pembroke Magazine: "And God Bless Harry"

Poem: "In Wyeth"

Poetry: "Birthday at the Motor Vehicle Dept.," "Bruegel's Players," "Eviction," "Going Under," "My Father's Story" (as "Hands"), "Inis Meáin," "Jocie at Advent" (as "Jocelyn at 87"), "Ladders to Glory," "An Old Man's Sense," "Rendezvous in a Country Churchyard," "Rescue," "Small Life Rising" (as "Ascension"), "The Tracking," "Twelve"

Poetry Daily (on-line)*:* "An Old Man's Sense," "Bruegel's Players," "End of the Season," "Learning the Angels," "We All Fall Down"

Poetry Northwest: "Baptism," "Signs"

Puckerbrush Review: "Getting Religion"

Prairie Schooner: "Company," "Last Minute"

The Recorder: "St. Gregory of the Golden Mouth"

Southwest Review: "Sudden Weather" (as "A Sort of Summer Storm")

The Southern Poetry Review: "Dance" (as "Balancing"), "First Snow in the Garden of the Geishas," "Moving Mother"

Tar River Poetry: "Your Things"

The Texas Review: "An Astonishment and an Hissing"

Verse Daily (on-line): "The Rector's Wife"

The Yale Review: "The Undoing"

Yankee: "Ceremony, Indian Summer" (as "Indian Summer"), "Coasting," "The Digging," "Greenhouse" (as "New England Greenhouse")

The following publishers issued books in which poems from this collection appear: The Texas Review Press (*An Astonishment and an Hissing,* 1983); William L. Bauhan, Publisher (*North Northeast,* 1985); Swallow's Tale Press (*We All Fall Down,* 1988); Antrim House — *Counting to Christmas,* 2002; *Learning the Angels,* 2003; *Passage,* 2004; *Private Collection,* 2005; *Getting Religion,* 2005; *First & Last,* 2006; *North Northeast,* 2nd edition, 2007).

"Ceremony, Indian Summer" won First Prize in the 1999 *Yankee* poetry competition. "An Astonishment and an Hissing" was awarded the Ruth Fox Award of the Poetry Society of New England and was part of a chapbook by the same title which received the Texas Review Chapbook Prize. *We All Fall Down* won the 1986 Swallow's Tale Poetry competition, judged by David Bottoms. "Skunk Cabbage" was broadcast nationally in 2001 as part of National Public Radio's *Weekend Edition.*

Special thanks to the National Endowment for the Arts and the State of Connecticut for fellowships that facilitated the writing of poems in this collection, and to the Wadsworth Atheneum of Art for permission to reproduce Andrew Wyeth's "Northern Point."

There are many to thank for aiding and abetting me as a poet, so many that I can't thank everyone. The poetry community in Connecticut has been enormously supportive. In particular, friends like Steve Foley, Pit Pinegar, Pam Nomura, Hugh Ogden, Gray Jacobik, Dick Allen, Norah Pollard, and Sue Ellen Thompson have been my constant support. And members of my family, especially my wife Sarah and son Robin, have given indispensable advice, as have the River's Edge Poets: Elizabeth Kincaid-Ehlers, Drew Sanborn, Charles Darling, David Holdt and Susan Lukas. Finally, I want to acknowledge two poets who have given me much encouragement over the years: Eamon Grennan and Richard Wilbur. This book is dedicated to all of you and to my starters: my mother, who set me on my journey into poetry, and my father, who blessed it in the end. Thank you. It has been a wonderful journey.

The Weathering presents many new poems, although they do not appear in a separate section but have been combined thematically with poems from my previous books, which have been considerably revised and rearranged. In short, this *New & Selected* is new in several respects. Composing it has felt much like composing a book-length poem. The process has been a joy, for which I owe thanks to Dick Allen, who suggested my somewhat unorthodox approach.

Rennie McQuilkin
Simsbury, CT
January 13, 2009

TABLE OF CONTENTS

I. MORNING

II. LEARNING THE ANGELS

III. SUDDEN WEATHER

VII. SMALL LIFE RISING

VIII. BESTIARY

IX. PRIVATE COLLECTION

Defenseless under the night
Our world in stupor lies;
Yet, dotted everywhere,
Ironic points of light
Flash out wherever the Just
Exchange their messages:
May I, composed like them
Of Eros and of dust,
Beleaguered by the same
Negation and despair,
Show an affirming flame.

W.H. Auden
"September 1, 1939"

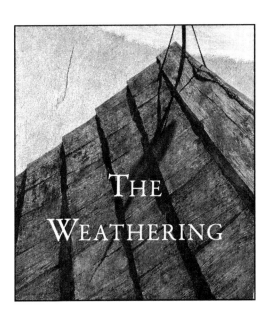

THE
WEATHERING

MORNING

MORNING

Lying alone in the straight and narrow bed
of old age, I work my way down the crooked hall
of memory—to where it was I went those early mornings,
trailing behind me the tattered cloudbank of my blanket

to the room Father had not yet expelled me from,
the room with the queen-size bed and rose-red comforter
I slid under, as close to Mother as possible, molding myself
to the seed-curl of her back and shoulder, the sweet tang

of her, slowing my breathing to match her own
with long, delicious inspirations
until first light lit the cream of her neck and cheek
and day broke in

with the rustle of pheasants in the pine,
fee-bee-ing of chickadees, *phew-phew-phewing* of cardinals,
swish of washing and brushing from
the street-cleaning truck

and finally the bellsound of bottles
set in their metal basket by the Nakoma Dairy man.
And Father would groan and Mother would turn to hold
me against the soft of her

and beyond the veil of her hair the light would grow and
she would take me by the hand along the dark crooked hall

to the back stairs, down to the bright kitchen,
and let me bring in the milk.

I'd uncrinkle the stiff paper cap of a narrow-necked bottle
and lift the tab beneath,
pull it from the mouth, love the liquid labor
and *pop* of its release

and lick the cream from its underside, the thick sweet cream,
a memory I knew—but not of what.

And God Bless Harry

After I godblessed everyone
and mother left
I godblessed Harry Walker

because when the air raid siren
wailed and Miss Berger rushed us
down past Harry at attention
in the furnace room

and lined us up
and made us sit small as spuds
and hug our knees,

I knew the Luftwaffe wouldn't
because Harry winked at me
and made circles around his ear.
And he would know—

the way he did when Miss Berger
sent me to the principal
and Harry stiff-armed his *Heil*
with a push broom under his nose
and a wicked grin for principals.

The last time I saw Harry Walker

they had him in a crib.
He couldn't move a thing.
But his eyes made circles
and I knew he had them licked.

BAPTISM

after "Baptism in Kansas," John Steuart Curry

Things keep going on the way they do
except one day in the middle of nothing
they don't.

I remember how hot it was—not a creak
from the windmill
and the Fords our folks had come in
steamed.

We stood around.
Our pockets were no place for hands,
they said, and wouldn't let us in the dark
of the barn or anywhere God wouldn't be
because the preacher was in the yard
to baptize whoever he could
in Tatums' water tank.

Six lined up.
I envied them the cool of their gowns
and the year or so they had on me
but not the way he dragged them under
and kept them there so long they bucked
like bullheads.

Mostly, I went along with the hymnbook

someone pushed at me
until he got to Ellen McGee,
held her under and didn't stop,
thinking maybe anything that pretty
was bound for goings on.

I was ready for something like the cat
I had tried to drown and failed
when up she came as sweet...
and stood for a spell at the edge
of the tank, at home in the sky.

And her gown, wet through, was true to her
and her face was where the sun had been.

THE ZENITH

for Brendan Burns and Jesse Case

Always the tall dark of the barn
to hide in, the mattressing
alfalfa, timothy, meadow grass.

Beyond the hickory stanchions
smooth as well-worked leather
from a century and more of cows,

beyond the Jerseys,
their mouths full of summer,
I climb a ladder to the mow,

from there to the cupola, a rope.
Like any raccoon I settle down.
It all comes in clearly now:

a gabbling of frogs in the swamp,
a hoot owl in the pines,
June bugs banging the Coleman

and maybe 50 stations on a Zenith,
an old one shaped like a church
I've put together tube by tube.

Wired to the Cooling Room

and grounded on the handpump,
that Zenith brings in

the Tigers, the Indians, the Pirates.
One by one I call them up,
in touch with everywhere.

THE NAMING

The summer I was twelve I began to know
the Bottom—old-growth sycamore and locust
thick with furred and gnarling vines.
I dug root-raftered burrows in mud-hole banks,
bushwhacked my way

to a clearing and something more,
bark on its logs, guinea hens on its roof,
a sow with one eye open under it,
and rocking on the stoop, smiling crookedly

at the little savage come up from the Bottom,
a man who said *Huh*. That summer I learned
to grain the guineas, slop the hogs,
kick the sow in the snout for chewing my boot,

bait hooks with crayfish, pull in bullheads,
slice off their barbs
and gut them with a single scoop of the hand.
I wore a crow's feather in my hair,
sometimes a cat bird's, once an oriole's,

told no one
how Henry Minor taught me
to fox-bark, fire only once, cry the creature's
treble death cry, see the fox ghost hover

and ask of it a blessing.

Then school began and he got work
raising a suspension bridge between two states.
I didn't hear from him the year he was gone
and when he returned, he slurred
and turned away.

By now I was occupied with being thirteen
too much to mind. Who was he anyway?
Some drunken Indian. He deserved
the bottle-bomb I set off in his outhouse.
When he fired at me, I couldn't forgive him.

Or myself. Or whoever tore down his shack.
Or how he vanished and fifty years passed
before he surfaced in the obit it took
for me to start forgiving both of us. It's time
I called him by his proper name.

Cries Like A Fox,
come from where you hide at the wood's edge,
name me, tell me who I am, give me back
my feather of Crow,
feather of Cat Bird, feather of Oriole.

THE PASS

Plato put it well, like so:
beyond the particular is the permanent.
That is, beyond the arc of one dead jay I throw
to the woods (it hits a pine
and drops),

beyond such a broken arc
and the almost parabolic piss Davy Miller took
at recess and hit the drinking fountain
and got sent to Miss Ward,

beyond such arcs
is the one they all aim to be.
I think I saw it in November of '53.
It was the Blue against the Brighton 2's,
fourth quarter, tight,
when Number 3, George Nichols of the Blue

faded back in the mud, back
to the end of his own end zone
and got one off as he went down. It spirals still
to the 50 and into the arms of the wide end
who fakes and cuts and pulls it in, a peach.
He hardly has to look for the ball.

Behind him Nichols is down, his number's mud,
but what he threw
was just what Plato knew he would.

HOME BURIAL

for J.L.C.

A boy is in the field, digging a hole,
whose father has been stunned by
the sledge of time, doesn't know

enough to drop or try again.
A boy is in the field, digging
a hole which is perfectly square,

whose father makes nothing true,
not his crooked furrows, swayback
barn, pretty wife.

A boy is in the field, digging
a hole which is perfectly square,
knowing all,

whose father didn't know enough
to keep old Moses from
bloating himself on half-ripe oats,

couldn't find the slugs
to shoot the horse
and had to use a maul.

A boy is in the field, digging

a hole which is perfectly square,
knowing all too well

how his mother once swung him
flat out in the spinning world
and said she'd never let go, ever.

A boy is in the field, digging
a hole which is perfectly square,
knowing all too well who it was

he saw,
skirt up in the mow
with the hired man.

A boy is in the field, digging
a hole which is perfectly square,
knowing all too well all he can do

is make it deep,
straight down enough
for more than a stiff-legged horse.

LINES

for Richard

It's only glass
I've broken. Mother goes on
licking a thread, pushing it at the eye,
face bunching like a club,
then heaves out of her chair and begins

to hit me
with a magazine, and when that shreds,
with her fists.

I can't forgive my father
for hiding
behind the paper, a big man twice
her size. As usual, he lets her happen,

doesn't say a thing.
She does the talking in that house.
My father is her cross, she says.
I can't forgive him
for not knowing better

and hide in the shed among the tools.
Today, he comes for me, has nothing
to say, just shows me
to the car. We reach the river

and in the trunk beside his rod
I find a brand new Heddon Tru-flex
with a Shakespeare reel. From his tackle
he selects a Green Ghost for himself,
Royal Coachman for me.

How delicately, with a huge hand
battered and missing a finger, he threads
the silk through the shining eyes
and ties the Royal to my leader.

All afternoon we work the trout.
The only sounds
are those that slowly grow used to us
and the high song, long whisper
of lines.

First his, then mine, then sometimes
together, the lines arch out, and settle
exactly where we want them.

MY FATHER'S STORY

One of his hands held the pulpit hard,
grew livid every Sunday.
The other aimed at the faithful.
Back and forth it would rake us,
mowing us down.

Like Abraham with Isaac overhead
my father held the Host, then broke it.
The wafer, snapping, might have been
me, held up, an example.
Of course it wasn't. It was God.
Over and over God broke
beneath his hands.

Nothing stood up to him.
When a cougar stopped our Franklin
ten miles beyond Carmel,
slow as the switch of the animal's tail
he reached for the tool box
on the running board, and the cat
backed off, didn't like the looks
of a hand that religiously raising
a hammer.

Moving east in '15, held up by snow
in the Sierras, my first,
we all got down from the Pullman.

I said it was Heaven
and I was an angel and could prove it.
Flat out, I made wings in the snow
and sang the Alleluiah Chorus.

When I turned to take my punishment
there were iceballs in both his hands
and two in the air.
He was juggling, juggling snow,
as sure of where we were as any angel.

FATHER'S HANDS

After work when the big and little hands
pointed opposite ways, he would listen
to the silver cocktail shaker he shook
just enough not to *bruise the gin*
and would down his three martinis
while I waited for him to hear my news.

Promptly at seven, dinner. A good wine
and he'd warm to the stories he told
more fashionably than any conversation.
Then Bach, his fingers
trembling on the strings, eyes closed,

after which he would disappear
behind the evening paper, the obits,
looking for news of his larger family,
the hundreds who worked for him.

Because I didn't,
I made myself small, tried not to think
how long it took him to see me
through the amber of a single malt

and tell me *Later.* Some nights he'd come
to my room, instruct me
with parables from his own boyhood, knead

my shoulders, ribs, the small
of my back—knead them sternly as if he
might be able to reform me.

SIGNS

Beyond my father,
splendid in his Lincoln Zephyr
making time cross country,
were the signs—

a sign for caverns miles deep where
fish swam with whiskers for eyes
and we'd get lost and I'd save us
with my length

of string, and one for Dinosaur Valley
where the bones would take on flesh
and backs like the Rockies
and tails to bash whoever I wanted.

Couldn't we stop, just once, to see?
And in the heat of noon he stopped
at a creek where he went in
with snakes and snapping turtles.

Later, my head on his lap
beneath the wheel, his thigh muscle
flexing and unflexing, I saw
him enter the ring

in scarlet tails and a silk top hat.
He flicked his whip
and two by two introduced things
too terrible not to be true.

WAR NEWS

At breakfast with father,
when I grew tired of seeing the war news
on the back of the paper he held, bare-
knuckled, I studied what else stood between us.

For all its British silver, it was Byzantine
and Gallic, onion-domed
and perforated with tiny fleurs-de-lis to
pour the sugar.

Or so I say now—
then, it was merely beyond me.
And he went on flipping pages with angry snaps.
Nothing worth his while there.

Still, the paper stayed up, the test
continued. I thought
of snatching the *Times* away, finding
my father

less furious
than disappointed I was, as ever,
stupid, stupid, stupid—like all the rest that
passed for news. So I waited,

watched his hand emerge, huge
and graceful,

close around the sugar tower,
raise it deftly out of sight behind the paper,

sweeten,
and return it, ridged and shining,
to its appointed place.
I made a promise to myself:

I would study harder,
craft myself more perfectly, wait patiently
for him to notice and reach out
that gently to me.

THE UNDOING

I jump from crosstie to crosstie,
walk a humming rail. This
is forbidden.

Rounding a bend I'm interrupted
by a barn
through which the tracks run on—
a heavyset barn, hand hewn,
with a long row of panes
like unbroken eyebrows
above the open double doors.

Within, a boy is about to get what's
good for him. His hands are tied
to a post, shirt off, pants down.
They're mine.

I hear the belt slip through
the loops, its slap against a palm
like stropping a razor, its whisper,
hiss, and crack.
What little I am is less.

Then there's no father, no buckle
shining like a badge, just the flash
of swallows, white of droppings.
The barn's roof is sagging,

slates broken.

I open a toolbox I'm never to open
and see no tools,
just thick red sticks I set so well
that when I trigger the barn
the fall of debris is gentle, a good
growing rain.

Moving Mother

Every spring she began again
to do her hair, legs curled beneath her,
nude at the heart of the garden,
flush terra cotta, too much the image

of my mother. Not for friends to see.
I was in favor of fall, leaves hiding parts
of her, and at last the removal—but not
the way my father held her,

taking her to the cellar, the pitch
black she wintered in—except for one
mica eye of the furnace
blazing, throwing light darkly on her.

What did I know? After he willed her
to me, I took her home
too carelessly, broke off a foot, a hand.

It's time I reconsidered
how she nestled in his arms.

LEARNING THE ANGELS

Twelve

for Robin

A pretty good day, junk fish
and a couple of trout.
Friendly with muskrat
I drift, I cast at rings,

pass the '58 Chevy with fins,
stripped, a place to play
in which I once found
underthings.

What's up
around the bend
is flowers, and among them,
reaching for the sky,

legs,
some girl's, toes curling,
curling, nails red, her hair
a sight. The boy I forget.

CECROPIA

It wasn't butterflies I went for, such daily flirts,
but moths, the shy ones, furred and thick-fronded,
pale green, lavender, umber, and rose-mottled
giants signed with the Eye of God.
Polyphemus, Promethea, Luna, Io, Cecropia.

Luring such mystery with a lantern
the summer I was thirteen, I saw across the street
the bride, moon-white, bridesmaids pale green
dancing in the gold and navy night.

At sixteen I kept a harem of cocoons, their silk-
sacks swelling, also a '51 Victoria convertible,
cow-horned, coral red.

The day I was licensed I floored her
on NY 96, Ruth Ferguson drumming our song
on the dash. Gearing down for the turn
onto Kreag, I backfired and backfired for Ruth,
who rose, leaned into the wind like a sprit,
her arms in the air in a V and her fingers V's
and the plunge of her two-piece—oh lord!

When I pulled in, late, a Cecropia had hatched,
was half eaten by ants.

They blackened its bright new fur,
the sockets where eyes had looked for some way
out of this, the pink and umber wings,
too wet to fly.

SOLSTICE

At the very instant of Solstice, when the sun stands still, all things
are at that Moment of Equilibrium when an egg will stand on end.

Nothing stands still this Solstice dawn.
Light lengthens on the bedroom ceiling, assuming
the form of a cross

with a bright amber square
at its crux. What physics is this? I'm used to
shadows—mullions and grackles.

A gilded blur begins to circle the top of the cross,
and the boy in me sees a perfect P-40 hung from
the ceiling, propeller pin-wheeling, glue still bright

where wings and body meet. The bishop in me
knows better—knows it's the Holy Cross,
the crux of it the terrible brilliance of an open heart.

Now the base of the Cross is dividing,
dividing again, becoming long side-by-side legs,
and the cross piece too is doubling, is blessedly

a pair of arms pinned
by another pair of arms. Nothing stays
still—the legs are twining

and her eyes are taking me in, brighter by the minute.

From the heart of us a light less amber than citron,
less citron than gold, is simplifying

whatever was merely human
until nothing is left of us but Light...
which slowly grows fainter, is gone—lets us down

to earth like anything perfectly upright declining,
falling, a moment after its Moment
of Equilibrium.

LEARNING THE ANGELS

Waiting up, he's deep in *Angels & Archangels*,
studying lion-bodied Cherubim, Principalities
six-winged, translucent as cathedral windows,
heavily armored Archangels, and the usual

angels for the dirty work, recording, hand-
delivering, and as he learns, placing a finger on
the lips of every newborn, leaving the cleft
imposing silence concerning clouds of glory.

Now she breezes in, douses the light, wants
to cuddle, undoes, runs a finger along the cleft
that gives the tip of his sex its face of a heart.
It's devil's work, he knows.

But here he is in the dew-damp garden at dawn
picking strawberries for her,
turning the leaves pale-side-up, uncovering
the heart-shaped fruit

and finding the snake, a hog-nose, head up,
neck flared and glistening. He knows its lineage,
says his prayer
to angels, archangels and wheels of fire.

Reinforced, he returns
full of Powers and Dominions. She yawns,

half rises on her divan, plumps a pillow,
pours cream on the berries. Its blush

deepens. He finds himself sliding a hand
beneath her robe,
along the nape, the shoulders, the spine,
the small, that valley lightly downed

which leads to what comes over him,
her shoulder blades working the air,
her finger on his lips.

Rendezvous
in a Country Churchyard

I'm early. I sit on Timothy Cowles,
d 1788, ae 41, and wait.
She'll be here soon:
the sun's not long for this world.
Meanwhile, Char ty How rd
depa t d in   r 3 th yr
is disappearing from her stone.

Over the Hales and Hopes,
the sons and daughters of the above,
their spouses and relicts,
sugar maples are all a mumble,
might be saying prayers for the dead,
except it's caterpillars:
the trees are half eaten, food for
worms with their prattle of scat
raining from leaf to leaf.

The usual mockingbird is at his
vireo, his bobolink and cardinal,
such pretty lies—like my lady's lips
and eyes, the skull's dress-up.

But soft, she comes, her lantern lit,

her face a lie I willingly accept.
She has me believing
the mockingbird's latest
is the very song of Charity Howard
delighting with Timothy Cowles.

DAWNING

Reflecting the moonshine
of a brewing bogful of peepers penny-whistling
and the fen toad's *woo-ah woo-ah* all night,

these two sleepers are out of themselves,
on tour, appearing in the dreams of one another.
When the nightly show is closed
by morning's pewter, blue, and lavender doves,

he feels the press of her finger on his lips
forbidding a word
of the world from which they're only half removed
here on this cumulus of sheet and pillow

from which he looks up—into the coming
of her eyes. About her disarray of hair, first light.

End of the Season

Scraping bottom, I pole us,
two old-timers,
through the gut to Turtle Pond.
Within, it's stop and go
and stinks. No place to bring you.

Think how it was in the spring,
I say—clear, the big snappers
gliding up like ocean-going Greens,
Pileateds scalloping the shoreline
red, white and black,
draping swags from tree to tree.

Whatever's left now is on its way
out—water lilies shut, olive drab
sepals stiff, a half-pint flask half
under, two mud-brown bobbers
mired—

all too apt. I'm at a loss, my love,
ship the paddle,
let the marbled algae have its way.

Is that you humming?
You like something so far gone?
I like how you chime in
with the splay-legged frogs

chirping, careening the scum,
how you let a slime of duckweed
and ooze of late bog-spawn
slide through your fingers
like a miser forgetting to count,
and how you sniff, connoisseur
of stinks.

But what do you make of this
that rises darkly to starboard now,
tows the swamp-green barge
of a shell, dangles the dead head
of a water lily from its jagged jaw,
inhales hoarsely

and sinks, slowly
until only the algae on its shell
protrudes like quills?

We know the stories—
mergansers, mallards, cygnets
going under with barely a ripple.

What you do
is reach out to rub it
with your paddle, and the old
snapper rubs back, revolving
so slowly counterclockwise

we lose track.

Next thing, it's dusk.
In the gut the rushes, feathered
beige, almost lavender
in the last light,
brush my neck, shoulders,
bare arms.

I like how you smile, reach back
to dub me with your paddle.

Ceremony, Indian Summer

an anniversary song

The afternoon ripens, the whip-poor-will
begins. Two dragonflies pause,
yellow-striped, red-tipped on a snag,
then blur to the pond,

resume their ritual, arched bodies coiled
tail to head and head to tail,
an eight-winged wheel of fire, a figment
from Ezekiel

above the bridal dance
of cloud-white, wing-furred caddis flies
redoubled by the pond.
Thistle seed drifts like confetti.

And deeper down in the angling light
past nubile perch in green and saffron
shallows, a pair of three-foot carp seem lit
from within

the color of the lingering sun,
their roiling in the rising mist of spring,
backs humped half out, snake-sinuous,
forgotten. The stillness of the carp

is so complete each red-gold, black-lined
scale shines separately, the pulse of tail fins
oriental, like the sway of night into day
into night.

AN OLD MAN'S SENSE

of time is shot. Now he is five in Indian headdress
facing off with the boy across the street
and now he is being born. The frames

blur by—his small head crowning, coming to light
is an old man's, white on hospital
white. Now the film so quickly reeling and unreeling

jams. It fixes on a single frame.
Before a brilliant circle burns out from its center
he sees

a sleeping compartment
elegant in the velvet and brass-fitted style
of the overnight express from Algeciras to Madrid.

He is raising a tasseled, dark green window shade
on the full Spanish moon. The white of it spills
across the cream and umber landscape of his bride.

SUDDEN
WEATHER

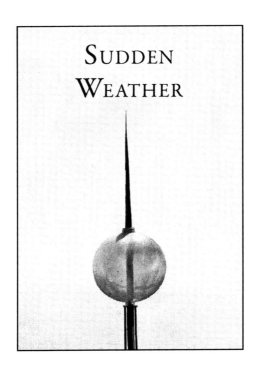

ELABORATION

for Robin and Will

Already four retaining walls are standing against
the tide. The builders have molded
the Ziggurat's tower and beyond it the Pyramid
of a Thousand Steps. When the sea rises

they rush to shore up the outer wall.
The more beach-goers gape at "two grown men
doing that," the more the couple's passion grows
for the pat-a-pat of sand.

It's a calling, like this I fulfill beneath
such darkening clouds—the prophet pointing
overhead, declaring Babylon
shall be rubble.

For their part, the lovers cover their ears
operatically. Now the sky over South Beach grows
more ominous, the wind quickens, thunderheads
light up from within, too much like

the Kingdom of No. They abandon all irony
for their final construction,
its Byzantine dome encircled by what
appear to be flamboyant seraphim, swords raised.

SUDDEN WEATHER

I can live with hurricanes,
their predictable haunts and
habits, established names.

But there's a sort
of summer storm,
a blackness out of the blue,

a whiplash
of wind, an end of more
than power.

And what of us? Against
whatever fury
has brewed in you for days

I lay in provisions, secure
all entryways.
I ride out rage, remain.

It's sudden weather
in the midst of love
will be the end of us.

Break Up

for D.W.

It's a godsend, this winter thaw,
I tell my brother, long distance.
He answers such warmth's unnatural.

When he asks how long it's been
since she left me, I'd say I have no idea
but am interrupted by a rumbling

from Smuggler's Notch. Which grows.
Now, where the creek clears the ridge
trees are cracking

and a blue-white flash flood of break-up
ice cuts through, shaking the house,
and veers off,

leaving a stand
of river birch in ruins beneath a wrack
of ice that glitters jade and silver.

When I can hear again, I hear more
clearly the small voice on the other end.
Forever, I say, *she's been gone forever.*

It's Been a Long Long Time

Mold and mildew. Beneath the kitchen sink
long pink and white shoots, beige-furred,
grow out of the eyes of Golds and Idahos.
Also the doorbell's dead, the pipes are bleeding
blue in the tubs, the water pump keens,
the roof leaks, the whole house is going soft.
I take it personally.

And there's the business of the light
in the upstairs hall
where the family is hung, two whole rows
of framed stiffs
coming out, coming down the aisle, going off
to war. No doubt the fixture I've just installed
will overheat like the last one
and with a sizzle and flash leave our forebears
in the dark. So it goes.

While I wait for Sharples the Chimney Man
to return, let me fill you in. A week ago
our Little Godin began to smoke us out
but before the coal gas caused total obscurity
Sharples fixed us up with a 5-inch insert
and a 9-foot extension that towers over the house
like the Newark incinerator—and doesn't work.

What else but retreat to *The Valley of Horses?*

Better Ayla than the flickering Zenith
where balding barbershoppers are carrying on,
crooning *Kiss me once and kiss me twice.*
Too close to home.

Thank God, he's back. Sharples.
He drills a hole in the stovepipe, inserts a gauge
to register the draft, and shakes his head.
Minus 2, minus 6, you have a negative draft, he says.
Doesn't make sense, he says. *She should draw
like a Hoover.* And here's the rub:
You must be in a natural low pressure zone.
I knew it.

He kneels before the stove,
says it's never happened to him before, pops a pill
from a bottle in his socket wrench box, departs,
does something on the roof
and reappears. He wads up paper, lights her,
and lo, we have to back off before she sucks us in.

It seems he has over-corrected. What to do
is his business. Mine is *The Valley of Horses*
where everything's new—and works.
So far Ayla has invented Fire, the Wheel, and the
Beast of Burden.
Just now she's about to invent, with the aid of

the first man she comes upon...

Before she can, my daughter walks in
with her young man. Interruptus once again.
He wants to call somewhere. I tell him to watch
the phone jack: it pulls out (how often I've lost
my party). *You have to click the tab on the jack,*
he says, with the patience of youth.

All right, I'm senile.
But when I've finished over-paying Sharples
I add it all up:

one light fixture, illuminating for the moment,
a working phone, a coal stove in the pink.
I can see, I can hear, I can feel—therefore I am,
I think I am, though the Zenith still flickers.

Before I lose my party once again, my love, I turn
to you. *It's been a long long time.*

ADMISSION

Hidden in the blind of my dream, I watch
Susanna naked in her grotto. The whites
of her teeth glitter, her black and secret fur

glistens. Then the otherworldly wail
of something
calls me

back to you beside me in bed,
your cries subsiding, the pain that stunning.
And now

at St. Francis Emergency, you bite your lip,
eyes wide. A young intern
pulls up your gown. Does this hurt, or this,

he asks, splaying your legs, pressing hard
where they meet.
A sharp cry seems to please him.

I know, it's his job. And mine is strangling
him, cracking his windpipe, until I come back
to you, or try—

I'm diverted by rain lashing, wind keening,
jumbo jets tossed about, unable to land,

according to the anchor on Channel 2.

What can anchor me?
I place a compress on your brow, rub you down,
concentrate on not composing this,

unsuccessfully. There is no health
in me. For which I hear the gurney coming to
cart me off to the underworld, but of course

it comes for you. They tape your ring,
explain the muscles relax under anesthesia,
rings fall off. More likely good pickings,

I think, and try to remember what ring
cynics are consigned to
and how much ring-loosening I'm guilty of.

Be true to her,
I want to tell the nurse who delivers
preliminary oblivion. His name tag says

"Angel." With that hush hush voice he's too
otherworldly. For one who doesn't believe
in signs, I'm surprisingly

terrified. How quickly you'll go spinning
into the dark

of the ether—

like this marbled earth, this bright new galaxy,
all of us on board,
brave running lights blinking, I write

and write. But what I want
is to pray
Please hold the instruments steady for her.

And now it's time to wait. Forever...
When they return you, they
are all you need, they and the morphine-trickler

you fondle between your breasts and squeeze,
making the trickler chime
like a fasten-seat-belt sign in one of the jumbos.

It reminds me
your long approach is far from sure.
Come in, my love, come in.

THE DIGGING

It's that time of year,
the hedgerows hung with bittersweet.
Potato time.

How early the freeze, I'd say
if we were speaking. We're not.
We turn our spading forks against

the earth. It's stiff,
the Reds and Idahos hard as stone,
a total loss.

Once it was us against the beetles,
blight, whatever was not potato.
How they flowered, rows and rows

in white. Now look.
We give it one last try, and there
far down in softer soil,

a seam of them, still perfect.
One after another
we hold them up to the dying day,

kneel down to sift for more.
In the dark of earth, I come upon
your hand, you mine.

RETROSPECTIVE

So many takes of Jo at Hopper's retrospective—
they say he married her for a permanent model.
Jo as hooker, nipples rouged, hair flaming with henna;
Jo hunched at a counter, night hawking;
Jo as wolf girl crawling into bed, nether fur licked
by the lecherous wind,
or naked at a gaping flophouse window.

Once, happily, she's Pierrette,
white ruff at neck and wrists, receiving applause
she deflects with a deprecating gesture of her hand
toward Pierrot, clearly Hopper himself
who touches his chest
as if before he can bring himself to respond

he feels an old weakness of the heart
keep him remote as the coast of Maine he loves
the way she wishes to be loved, wishes
so terribly she rages silently.
I understand. I too have earned such rage
though you keep it to yourself, my dear, as we go on
from Hopper to Hopper.

Now from a dark place behind *Two Comedians*
where a film shows every half hour,
a loud thud
is followed by strange soprano laughter,

no, not laughter—the ascending laceration
of a scream rising into a gasped series of *No's*.
Then the silence that follows a natural disaster.

Across the gallery your face is unmasked
in a shock so pure
it's a mirror for mine. How long
it has been since we looked at each other
so—not husband, not wife,
but true as only strangers thrown together are.

THE BALANCING

Rome: December, 1985

On my own this morning, lugging my bags
to the check-in counter, I'm just another
of her numbers. She works here
as a Balancer, measures baggage against jet fuel.

I clench my eyes, relive last night:
how she came back from the airport, late,
how I wanted her,
how she knocked my hands away, exploded
with fury. So much for us.

I look up, may be the last to know.
The arrival and departure screens are riddled,
glass crackles underfoot,
a pattern of blood designs the wall.

At Security the Carabinieri carry Uzis.
No one says a thing. On board, we frisk
each other's faces.

It fills the papers we hide behind:
there were four,
back to back in a circle. Grenades, 47's.
They weren't particular about their targets.

I turn a page, stare at Mohammed Sharam,
the youngest. Such a sad face.
He says they dragged his father from a loom
in Gaza, cut off both hands,
and while his sister knelt, head down
as if to Mecca, raped her.

The wheels slam into the belly of the plane.
We rise above the city. It simplifies, is lost,
the world turns white,
then silver, pale blue, reminding me

of the ice on Pemadumcook. I'll go there—
little cabin, nice fire. Cold nights the ice
explodes, but it harbors no fury,
no national cause. When a floe scrapes a floe
it sounds sound like cellos...

Still, I feel no peace.
Balanced between the old world and the new,
near the point of no return, I turn to her,

retrace her steps...
From where she works, she must
have seen it all, must have come home to
rest her head on me, whisper *No, oh God, no!*

I will try the one way home.

THE TRUTH
BEYOND US

HOME BIRTH

for Benjamin

The cord was about your neck
when you were born
blue. A spring blizzard raged.

You survived, and the weather
turned, but today four-foot drifts
are up to the bird feeder

where the cat digs in, hunkers,
and deep in her throat makes
bird noise: ruffles, clever trills.

The birds know, except a junco
comes close, too close.
The cat leaves it for me to end.

When I turn to you
my shadow darkens the crib.
You sound too like the bird.

I look elsewhere,
concentrate on the egg shine
of dawn I woke to this morning,

magnified wings silhouetted

on the window shade, hardly
celestial: starlings

in love with construction,
scratching snow from the gutter,
weaving a wattle of twigs, doing their

parody of whatever deconstructs—
rattle of snow plow, snarl of chain saw,
birdcall of cat. Such a razzing!

May a starling be your totem, Ben.
May false ruffles and trills have
nothing to do with you.

WE ALL FALL DOWN

for Kelly, my student

Her turn had come. She knew
by heart almost
the lines she was to speak
but gave us, God help her,

the truth
beyond the lines,
beyond the book she dropped,
its pages thrashing to the floor
like broken wings—

the truth
she beat her head upon,
bit into so hard
I could not pry her jaws,
teeth grinding—

the truth beyond us
she saw as ever,
her risen eyes gone white
as bone.

I did what I could,
I held her and held her, seized

with sudden love and knowing
we all fall down.

In the end
I carried her curled in my arms
across one threshold
and another.

BEYOND THE MYSTIC

for David and Beeke

He began building the boat when doctors gave me
a year, maybe two.

He used nothing but the best—bronze bolts,
white oak for the battens and gussets,
ironwood for the keel.

Now in the cool of evening, I ride
my name on the prow,
listening to the intermittent ping of the fish scanner.
We work a pair of poles.

He is taking me down the Mystic
to his favorite haunts, celebrating contradiction.

As we pass beneath the 99th St. Bridge,
the big trucks making their metallic thunder
on the perforated steel of the roadway above,
he selects another lure,
the lamp on his head less a miner's than a surgeon's:

the big one he pulls up amazingly
from such a place
will be a mystery, like perfect health.
Nothing doing, no bites—

a year, maybe two, time for my marrow to turn
white, bones riddled and cracking.

Where the Mystic opens
into Boston Harbor, we move on to deeper water
beside the Chelsea Power Station's
screech of steam, and pass a foaming spill
of superheated water. It draws the Blues, he says.

From the plant's many stacks
cold white, pale green, and deep red beacons pulse,
reflecting on the thickening mist and tidal eddies,
multiplying strangely. A searchlight scans the scene
like the pointer on an x-ray screen. Just beyond,

by a flood-lit construction site and the clattering
of scrap metal on a recycling plant's conveyor belt,
he has a strike, pulls in a striper, mauve-streaked,
not quite a keeper.

It has swallowed the lure. He cuts the leader,
holds the fish over the side of the boat, waits for a sign
of life, holds it a long time in the healing water.

Let go.
I am not what I was,
but I am
what I will be,
waiting for you, always here
just beneath the surface.

LOCKSMITH

Beyond a boarded up Richfield station
with its crumbling porte-cochère
and old glass-headed pumps, his sign:
Clocks & Toys Repaired, Locksmithing.
And underneath, in finer blue and red,
Country Quilts.

He lets me in through the kitchen,
gray-grizzled paunch
too much for his terry cloth robe.
Dishes overflow the sink.

He takes my suitcase, leads me
through the parlor.
In the half dark an open couch-bed,
someone in it.

Downstairs, his shop is immaculate,
a place where everything will work—
clocks, watches, bits of a tiny carousel
laid out precisely on a workbench.
Next to them is a jeweler's eyepiece.

Pulling up a chair to the suitcase
he whistles happily, runs a hand across
its hardware, shines a pen light on it.
Which gives him pause—

"This will be hard. She's a Marathon."

He jiggles a knife in the lock,
shakes his head,
takes key after key from a box, holds them
up to the light, shakes his head again, rises,
goes to a rack, runs a finger slowly down
his "blanks,"

pauses, reverses direction, and stops
at the space where the right one should be,
continues to point as if it might appear,
says that's the way it is—nothing he can do.

Returning, we pass through the parlor.
No sound from the bed, no definition,
but on the wall behind, a portrait
with its own small light—
dark hair, high cheekbones, green eyes
above a quilted shawl.

"Cancer," he says. "A month, maybe two."

From the dark of the driveway, I see him
enter the workroom, pick up the eyepiece,
put it down,
turn again to the wall of blanks.

THE HOLE

Night rises quickly up the canyon
walls. We are soon calling out
the names of constellations
crossing our narrow slice of sky

and point by point striking
a granite outcrop, disappearing.
At dawn I climb a rubble of scree
to the outcrop

where ravens clack beak on beak
as if to sharpen them,
their eyes the blue of anthracite.
Here, half hidden by yucca,

the glitter
of a three-foot shard of propeller.
It comes back—the faded fact
of a mid-air collision

is a bright flash, terrible silence,
loud report,
a piece of wing, a valise, a shoe
turning end over end. Far below,

the mud-red Colorado drowns
the turquoise of the Little Colorado

and the flood-swollen river leads to
"the Hole" at Lava Falls.

Our guide has never seen it so high.
By their tiny bone-white dories
my companions might be pins
marking the spot, thin spit of sand.

At the edge of the cliff, I lift
the prop, set its silver, blue, and red
upright in a wreckage of rocks.

LAST

in the Kuznetsk Alatau Mountains, Southern Siberia

He and she are old. They are dying. Perhaps not today
but soon, soon. They are in the way, a remnant
no longer protected by the deep pocket of their valley
to which the oil rigs have come, and drillers from Kiev,

whose word for him means "loco local."
He's unintelligible, bent like a Siberian birch from
too many winters. And she at ninety a chanter of the old
songs—in a language these two are the last to speak.

No matter. No one needs such words
as *pine smoke-fire for orchard frost.* Smudge pots do it
better. And sixty-one nouns for a dozen healing herbs
are pointless. The world has pharmaceuticals.

This is the way evolution works. It doesn't protect
what isn't needed, wipes it out,
tries something else, obliterates that,
starts again…

The universe has no use for the senseless song
she sings, cradling him at the foot of the apple ladder
from which he has fallen, or for a love-name he prolongs,
tracing like a blindman the map

of her palm, map unauthorized by the authorities, map
containing place names only these two remember,
map which he will not let go, even as his hand
falls away from hers.

So Much Mourning

is unreasonable they say
taking me where fish shacks
bloom on the ice
turquoise pink jade

and this year's contestants
tie lures to lines to flash
like chandeliers in the dark
fish parlors

inviting the big one
the winner
and the young go at it
their GMC's rocking the ice

but I hear just a drumming
below. Hollow thud of waves
on a ceiling of ice. Someone
trapped beneath a final lid.

I know—the ice will relent
and be a dazzle of lake and
bluegills with fish shack colors
will jump. But not now, not yet.

for Margy

THE MUGGING

She runs so hard she leaves herself behind:
high heels, a hat and coat line the sidewalk.
She's chasing the mugger.

He's lanky, raw, could outrun her easily
but not the way he ducks and dodges
as if the enemy
is everywhere, as if the street is mined.

When she grabs his shirt, he waves her purse,
white flag.
She follows through, knocks him
into the path of a bus.

Now two cops are trying to raise her
where she kneels,
his head in her arms, all around her a spill
of belongings. Nothing moves.

She and the man her hair half hides
are white as marble.

WILDFLOWERS

for Jocie

After visiting you, raised up on the bed
to breathe, the only color in your face
the dark of an open mouth
and a spot on the lower lip
where you must have bitten yourself—

after searching the whites of your eyes,
conceiving of your mind as blank
and admitting that nothing
will color it in,

I've come out here to remember you
in the field you loved. It's hard.
What was it you saw in these flowers?
They're all show,
hypocrites and liars, lippy little flirts.

Or worse, they're not, they're dying—
like the Queen Anne's Lace,
your favorite: blank white faces,
black spots at the heart,
that just a week ago were green cups
to catch the rain and hold the dew.

I'm wrong, of course.

In a quick wind
the Lace begins to sway, white gone
to shades of cream and pink and pale blue.
The dark at the center
is Tyrian. The Persians traded spice for less.

I'm bringing a handful to put by your bed.
It has a lovely scent—
like carrot. You'll remember.

THIS

SISTER MARIE ANGELICA
PLAYS BADMINTON

with Sister Marie Modeste most afternoons.
Today, because of lengthy vespers, they are late.
A pale moon has already risen and early bats
are darting like black shuttlecocks.

Except for the whisper of wings
and the Sisters' hushed encouragement,
the only sounds are the plinking of rackets
and a monotone of mourning doves.

On all sides of the court
the sculpted yew in cubes and columns
might pass for black so deeply green it grows.
And now it moves closer,

Marie Angelica would say,
who has been known to have visions.
Though she moves as aptly as the bats,
doesn't miss a shot,

when she fades for a long one
from Marie Modeste, sways on her toes, arches
her back, raises one arm
and the other to keep her difficult balance,

she is lost, a long-legged girl again

in mare's tail, mullein, milkweed,
leaning on the sudden sky as if it can sustain her
like a hand in the small of her back. It does.

Her nerve ends quick as a shiver of poplar,
arms like branches in a wind,
she feels a cry begin
to rise, to force the self before it

and burst, all colors one. That white.
It vaults straight up, a feathered cry
that hovers in the heart of heaven, hovers,
and plummets to the gut

of the racket she sights it in,
the perfect bird, the shuttlecock
Marie Angelica keeps in play, will not let fall
despite the darkness gathering.

after David Inshaw, "The Badminton Game"

THE REVEREND ROBERT WALKER SKATES

on Duddingston Loch at sunset
in black—black top hat and frock coat,
britches, garters, stockings, skating shoes
black. Except for pink laces
and the flush on his face, slightly deeper
at the ears,
he is black as this morning's sermon.

Oh yes, his scarf is white. And if I say the ice
is black, I mean it's not, is in fact
a window for fish.

The Reverend has turned his back on the sky
between the hills, which is the color of his ears.

His right leg is raised, extends behind him
like the long tail feathers of some exotic bird.
He is leaning into the wind,
leading with the sharpened blade of his nose,
arms wrapped one inside the other.

Or so Sir Henry Raeburn, R.A., did him
in oils, c. 1794.

Those fine cross-hatchings on the Loch
are not from all the Reverend's parishioners

celebrating after service, skating up a storm,
for the hills and the sky seem no less
skated upon.
It's Time. As surely as ice, oils crack.

Nor is the clerical top hat what it was.
You'll find the ghost of its earlier brim,
painted out imperfectly, is aimed low
as if a moment ago the vicar was searching
for a flashy trout.

He has, it appears, raised his sights
to the deepening blue of night, or something
more distant. He dedicates a miracle
to it, no major miracle, mind you, but still...

He makes his turn (notice the sliver of ice
kicked up by the heel of a skate),
has all but completed the figure 6
he means to raise
to an 8.

RIDING THE TIRE

The world's a bog. It's been raining, slowly,
grimly, for days. A good many things
have gone under.

If I'm still here as surely as there's life
in the grays and greens on soggy whole-wheat,
it's not my idea.

The radio comes and goes, announcing
lively disasters in foreign parts, and once
a steady, high-pitched whine

is followed by a tornado
warning for Berkshire and Hampshire Counties.
Never my own. All afternoon

I have seen the big blue-blacks go rumbling
across the north, have watched their distant
firing. I do not think they will fire on me.

In such an atmosphere
philosophy proliferates like cultures
in a petri dish.

My exit now from the softening house is
more like an absence of any refusal
to exit.

It's grisly in the east all right,
neither raining nor not.
But westward

how the willows glisten,
all those flashy little leaves like swallows
banking on the sun.

Even the balding tire dangling from the maple
is bright, every last statistic showing.
From its dirty trough

a Black-eyed Susan shines. I can do
no less, climb in, am rounded out. Higher
and higher I ride the tire.

THIS

Fresh from the elegant park at Coole
and the Celtic crosses of Connemara,
more at home in that other world
than here at Scrubby Neck,

I hear them again, close overhead,
see their crossing—the black swans,
necks stretching for the Gayhead cliffs,
wings whistling *this This, this This.*

KILLING TIME

Just out of sight of the bridge on Hungary Road
I'm killing time while my grandson casts
for trout too cagey to show their spots
where the water bubbles and eddies below a fall.

Beer glass glitters, a dirt bike mutters. No luck
here, and we move downstream.
Salmon Brook widens and deepens, is overhung
by a sycamore

kids must once have monkeyed up
to the fraying rope still dangling from a limb.
I find a sitting-stone, pull out the May number
of *Poetry,* and presently two damselflies

shift their affair from phlox to the written word.
One has white-spotted jet black wings
and an iridescent blue-green abdomen;
the other is dun but completes the circle

the first began by gripping her neck with his tail—
she bends a dusky abdomen up to his, strokes
seed from him with delicate and digital concern.
When every so often she pauses, his wings

blur. Clinging to page 86—oh flagrant delight—
the two are right over Eamon Grennan's

"free of memory and forecast." This is killing
time the way it ought to be,

not the way I counted knots on the swing-rope
a moment ago—like telling beads. Now
I see myself climbing the rope, knot by knot,
swinging, letting go with a cry, in love

with nothing but this. But no,
it's my grandson's cry. He has hooked,
amazingly, a many-colored Brown
that shimmies over the brook, shimmies and

backflips, is gone. And there the damselflies go
and there the dirt bike's back and traffic
is clicking on Hungary Bridge. What it tells
is time.

MORE THAN
I AM

INIS MEÁIN

Considering millennia of tooth and bone and carapace
drifting down in a nameless sea to pave
this barren land for boulders rolled by glaciers to inscribe,

considering the generations that hoisted
the scribbling stones to wind-breaking, wind-wailing walls
to story the land, scratched up what little soil welled

in cracks, hauled seaweed, goat dung and pulverized rock
in sally baskets tumped to brows to cover
the old stone text with loam—considering such

revising, I am more than I am who in a minor plot today
plant rhyming rows
of seed potatoes, withered things, and pray
they will translate well, bloom white as tooth and bone.

AFTER WATERLOO, WHAT

he engineered were parapets of dirt
around the perimeter of his empire at Deadwood
to fend off the madding trade winds and the eyes
of the English, how many hundred English
to keep him in his desert enclave on St. Helena.

Inside the parapets he saw to the installation
of a formal garden sufficient to halt the advance
of an enemy more clever than his witless jailors.

When the hundred peach trees of the promenade
wilted, canaries in the aviary and koi in the pool
keeled, and the pièce de résistance, imperial Eagle
made of local clay
had the wings hung out to dry of a cormorant,

he had to laugh that charmingly rueful laugh.
The worst was the fountain that sputtered like
an old man's seed. He disappeared for days.

And still—
throughout the summer of 1820 guards saw
the bloated Emperor (no one suspected arsenic)
wielding a watering can at 5 a.m.
in his tattered nightgown and dirty red headband.

Barely able to walk, he persisted

in irrigating his pennyroyals, passion flowers
and seven kinds of rose.

He called the first his Marie-Louises, the second
his Josephines, the rest his Little Ladies.
They would never remarry, carried on no affairs,
told no one of his "difficulty." They were all
the forces he had left

to fight the enemy—not the assassin who laced
his white Bordeaux with arsenic
but the sot who knew the poison by heart
and drank it gladly.

THANKSGIVING, FIN DE SIÈCLE

Her timbers creak like the century
when she pulls herself up from her recliner for reasons
she forgets and shuffles painfully, gripping the arms
of her walker, as once she held—whose arm was it,

she wonders, shuffling from room to room—so many
photographs of men in uniform and ladies in waiting
for them to return, ladies
in veils for grief, for weddings, for reasons she forgets,

and pictures of children, grand and great
grandchildren, all the same. Are they her dream
or she theirs, and where is whatever she left behind
to get wherever she is,

and why is she in the midst of so much
empty space she wishes would shrink, enclose her
like a mahogany box with a ceiling of silk like clouds,
like—

No she doesn't. She takes it back. One foot goes
before the other, and there it is, she remembers now,
the recliner. She has made the circuit.
Thanks be.

FLOWER FARMER

Last fall Mr. Dewey wrapped his house
with sheets of plastic.
Lit by headlights, it glittered red and blue.

This spring it lists farther, the shingles flap,
and you can hear, he says, the tick
of water dripping, termites, beetles, mice.
As for his greenhouse, it's held up by vines
and sprouts patched stovepipes crookedly.
All winter Mr. D "cooked dirt" for potting.

He's out of sorts today.
She's dead, the '58 DeSoto that pumped river
to his flowers. Still, it's spring,
his dentures sparkle,
he's in better shape than that neighbor of his
with the heart thing,

and there's always the granddaughter.
She's a one with glads,
a natural with 'lips and daffs
but a little wild for boys, he's glad to say—
plant her here, she comes up there.

Putting in carnations this morning
he found another arrowhead.
Onyx, an ornamental. He looked it up.

Ask to see his Indian stuff, he'll ask you in.
Old man smell and mildew and dry rot
and catstink and African violets everywhere,
furry as an old man's ears.

He has, he says, the Indians cold—
knives, scrapers, axes, mauls.
He's proudest of a three-foot pestle stone,
the tip worn smooth.
According to the museum man
it was hung from a sapling to pound seeds.

He can see it now. She's something,
the girl who works the pestle stone.
A sapling pulls it up, the maiden pulls it
down, sapling up, maiden down,
grinding lilyroot.
From her face the granddaughter grins.

Mr. D is bent
like a birch the pestle stone's done with.
But he raises the stone overhead, in love
with whatever works. Damn DeSoto!

The Institution of Seed

for the scientists of the Institute of Plant Industry,
Leningrad, 1941-1942

The siege began with bombardment.
Leningrad on fire turned our smoke-smothered days
blood-red. Breathing came hard. Stone and dirt
blossomed when Nazi shells fell short in the fields.

And still we continued to harvest. When one of us
was hit, bits of limb and torso staining the sky,
we made ourselves go on

digging seed potatoes from mounded ridges
too like the raised earth above so many newly dead.
We were that desperate, digging up

pure strains of every known variety, preserving
what our fathers' fathers and theirs for generations
had cultivated—

the long white baking potatoes, round red Nevskies
and saffron Lugovskies, saved against a disaster
worse than war. Replanted every year,
not one should be lost, whatever else might be.

All winter, we lost. Shells falling on St. Isaac's
blew out the Institute windows. And the mercury

also fell—winter of '42 was the coldest on record.
No wood or coal got through the blockade,

so we burned what we could, floorboards, chairs,
to keep from freezing
the tons of heirloom seed—wheat, corn, rice,
and seed potatoes.

In January, rats invaded. We shifted the seed to
ammunition cans, beat back the rats with
whatever hadn't burned. But that other gnawing

of hunger! And the fury of that other beating—
hundreds beating pans beyond our walls, drumming,
drumming for food. What sustained us was belief

in a day more terrible when the seed would be all
that could save humanity, a day we had to hold
up against those faces, gaunt, accusing—
like our own.

We too, bones surfacing, had little time left.
One morning we found Dimitri Ivanov dead at
his desk, frozen.

Cradled between his arms
were dozens of packets of rice, a rare variety he'd

kept from freezing. Not a packet was open.

In March those of us left
sent as much of our stock as we could
by late night runs across the ice of Lake Ladoga
to caves in the Urals.

That summer, we knew, a mountain field would
blossom white and pink with potato
for posterity.

THE SON

It's quiet out here in the barn. There's time to think
how six hundred acres came to be worth
a quarter what I paid,
soy beans, feed corn rotting in the field,

and how I couldn't see what I was up against—
except Aloysius Hammer, come out from the bank
to say *Sorry, Tom, but no, not this time.*

The auctioneer was Jay Kyle, Roy's son.
Three counties showed up.
Someone was selling beer and franks,
and during breathers Ike Kassit played his fiddle
until my brother cracked it.

It wasn't just equipment and stock
but the linen tablecloth, china, loveseat, every stick
we owned, and a piece of Abbie with each.
She wouldn't come near me, hid the boy behind her.
They gave us a week to leave.

As I said, it's quiet out here. The air at least
is slow to rush in, leaves space
where they were—the Deere, the Harvester,
nine hundred pounds of sow, a mowful of timothy.

The cool eye of the Smith & Wessen is a comfort

I hold to my head.

What stops me is column on columnn
of head marks, white lines by the door to mark us
at ten, twelve, fourteen. We're all there,
my father taller than his, his son beyond him
by a head, my Jim three inches more last year alone.

And this—framed by a hole in the siding,
the headstones on the hill, each looking over those
before it. That much at least belongs to me
and an easement out to tend the graves.
It's time I did.

DANCE

After your first chemo we head for the shore
where summer after summer you danced
from Green Hill to Galilee before your fortune
turned to bearing, raising, then this.

At dead low we reach the rock-cobbled mudflat
at Matunuck, discover the mussels have vanished,
even the smallest hacked off by lubbers
from shacks and RV's multiplying extravagantly.

In the heat of late afternoon, we wait out
low tide, give the surf—and surfers, if any
are left—time to ride in where boulders begin
to heave the sea to rip-curls.

And now they come, as ever, with neon boards,
balancing, balancing, riding the crest above
the dark below.
We concentrate on the art of it.

SUTTEE

In the heat of the pyre
his right hand rose and curled to a fist.
I waited for them to throw me beside him.
They avoided me.

Since then I have burned
with a fury
so forbidden my hand shakes even now as I write
how he rewarded

the scantness of my dowry—
took me quickly on our wedding night,
smothered my face with the bridal gown,
bruised my throat,

the scream with which he finished
the same I heard from him in the servants' quarters.
Too many of their children
have his jaw.

The ashes still warm, his younger brother took me
to Brindavi, City of Widows.
The women in threadbare saris held out
their pittance bowls

as I would not.
I found my way to serve Krishna

in the Temple of Satyana-ra-yana, dancing for Him
to the beat of the tabla,

the drummer's hands a blur
my limbs desire. I am slowly learning the uses of my
self, may someday be able to ring
however many of my hundred ankle bells I wish.

CATHEDRAL FIRE, 1956

And the Lord went before them by day in a
pillar of cloud...and by night in a pillar of fire.

Exodus, 13:21

When I got there, St. Joseph's was
too far gone to be saved—
a column of smoke from afar

and closer,
a pillar of fire.
Then the rose window blossomed,

exploded. A whirlwind arose
and from the belfry, bells,
bells ringing their terrible changes.

As the organ fell
from the choir loft to the nave,
the battering, the heat, something

set it chiming,
playing its sharps and flats
in a fugue of its own creation.

May you and I go down
with such an explosion of music,
a song of songs.

for Fran

SMALL LIFE
RISING

JOCIE AT ADVENT

She no longer goes out, does little
to the dust which falls and falls
like snow in the globe of glass
she turns this way and that.
    Oh the bright little people within,
    their ageless sleigh, their song.

It is the season
for candles, one in every window.

She lights one for her father,
how little he weighed at the end,
how slight the skin which kept life in.

And one for the Morgan
who steamed like a field in his pride,
went lame, half blind, in the end
was dragged off by a tractor.

And a candle for herself, her dust
as brief as snow in a globe of glass.
    But such bright little people within,
    their ageless sleigh, their song.

She rocks and waits

for the light to flicker, waits
for darkness like the lake she dove
as a child.

    Oh the bright little stones
    below, the aggies and cat's-eyes,
    their glimmer in the dark.

Training the Eyes

for Jocie Sloan and Alex McQuilkin

Walking straight to the river with Alex
on my shoulders, hands reining me,
turning my head, is better
than so much circling of the fact:

Jocie has gone under, will not recover.
We stop where the river turns back
on itself, dangle our feet from the bank,
consider the current.

I watch the confusion
of the surface, a caddis fly fluttering,
then floating like Ophelia.
Alex sees it

otherwise, says the river is a fish.
At first I don't, then do see shadows
of leaf wrack and caddis fly,
magnified, riding the amber river bed:

the spots of an enormous trout.
Now the current slurs
like someone stricken straining

to speak. I could almost believe.

Say again, Jocie, how your father
took you, new born,
to the barn to touch the nervous flank
of Sirro the Arabian—to live forever.

SWIFTS

for Arlene Swift Jones

About this ring of friends, gravestones gray with age
are stamped with rose and verdigris patches of lichen
round as medals. An honor guard salutes.
Three rifle volleys.

Above us, against storm clouds still flicking the last
of their lightning, wings swirl,
hundreds initialing the sky, white and whiter on gray,
then veering, vanishing darkly

and reappearing, dazzling, turning as one.
Now two break off, coupled in upward spiraling,
and now they rejoin the collective...
A rain of dirt brings me back to earth, to a gap in it,

back to Arlene throwing in
the first handful. She sways toward the gap, and back,
and toward it.

I think of the swifts,
how their formation will funnel
into the four-square darkness of their nightly roost
from which at dawn they'll burst as if the light is all.

VALENTINE

for James Merrill, 2/13/95

Bright, almost St. Valentine's, the day the bells
of your village tolled
to say the Spirits had claimed their most telling
translator. Tolled, that is, as you would have them.

How like you, JM (who insisted
on your purple, starred kimono and crimson slippers
for the occasion of your incineration)
to have the bells, like the heart of a bride, beat so

quickly, and to chime in, once removed, so merrily
in your ex's elegy
concerning his latest amorous catastrophe
thus—"My dear boy, have you considered a corgi?"

"Or tulips?" I could hear you add. You loved
it all. And let us in on it. Small wonder
that after your newest beloved,
kissing your ashes, swept down the aisle, rushing

you to the softly purring limo, I saw at the tip
of my cramp-toed shoe, mundane planchette,
the twinkle of a coin, two bits,

as if in passing you'd tossed it off, new-minted,

a quip to counter mortality, or the bride's bouquet.
P.S. Having seen you to your digs, I made my way
down to your harbor where the swans let loose
with grunts and whistles. How little, JM, was mute.

SMALL LIFE RISING

for Gladys Egdahl

Left behind, I've followed her
to this windy height in the hills of West Virginia.
Under a rattling canopy
I shiver, listen to the Word, hear praises sung.

Her cherry box is poised on slings above a gape
too like her open mouth those days she lay there
waiting, dark gargle rising in her throat.
I look away.

Overhead, a Red Shoulder riding the wind
is not, of course, what I wish it to be.
A hawk's a hawk, focused
on matters of moment—milk snake, rabbit, vole.

The box sways on its slings, the winch grinding
out of sync with the Twenty-third Psalm, and there
she goes. Dear God, my mind is
slipping.

Let me think—of anything—of the underground
deposit of salt that made this town—
river water superheated to steam, pressured
down through sixty feet of shale to melt the salt,

the brine pumped back (hue of the death collecting
in a dun deposit on her lips)
to evaporating tanks, from which the fine white
salt of West Virginia came. How good to believe

her bones will rise no less, sluff death and shine
in their dance. Now the box hits bottom bluntly.
I'm brought up short, in time for the dive of the hawk,
the kill, the small life rising, completely loved, reusable.

MARK'S AUTO PARTS

In come the wrecks to Mark's
and out the gear knobs, gas tanks,
radiators, speakers, mufflers.
Bins of parts.

The crummiest clunker is worth
Mark's while. There's an alley
of front ends—Beetles, Buicks, Jags,
a '49 Nash,

an avenue of chassis,
a park of gutted bodies piled on
one another like lovers. Everything has
a future.

All of which is very gratifying, a sign
of what we'll amount to
in the after time.

The loosestrife will take this, frogs
that, the earth will value
our humus, the cardinal put us to use.
Dismantled, we'll go far.

BESTIARY

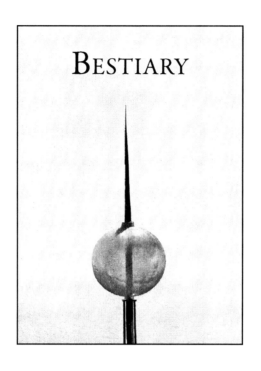

Greenhouse

Nothing doing here, no
goings on in this gray
greenhouse

whose heaven is broken
bits of glass the rats
translate to sand.

The gears that opened it
with a well-oiled hum
are frozen.

What was a garden
is a whistle for
wind,

snow curls in the corners,
and rust's half through
the furnace

from which a sapling
heads strictly for
the clear-cut sky.

Valley of the Naugatuck

After winter's discontent, I love
how you stretch out, rising and falling
as I near the heart of you,

your scents lush in the slick of rain:
wry aromas from last year's leaves,
umber from the mud,

sweet from syringa, shadblow, cherry,
lubricious from the musk, discreet,
of a skunk—

love how this scrim of rain
refines flamboyance to the subtle hues
of an Utamaro courtesan,

each washing into each—
how pleat by pleat your hills open
to whitewater muscling darkly through.

The who's who of high school love
(sad tall tale spray-painted on a bluff)
is muted by mist. It's what I'd have it be.

SKUNK CABBAGE

A rattle of winter-stiff grass in the field,
and in the sheep shed
a ewe, mother-mumbling deep in her throat,
two lambs still orange with birth.

The ewe is busy licking the larger, butting him
toward a teat, paying no attention
to the other in a corner,
giving up.

It's all quite peaceful, this dying.
Already the ewe, as she licks and butts,
is scratching a trough to which to nudge what
didn't work out.

I rub the runt angrily, press his mouth
against a nipple, knead his neck
to start the swallowing,
and force the milk—

too fast. He chokes, eyes bulged,
and from the nose, small bubbles, unbroken.
It's an act. I tell the legs to kick, the eyes
to look lively. They don't, they mean it.

Digging a grave at the edge of the bog,

the muck in love with my shovel, sucking it in,
down I go.
How lovely, the dark…

And from below, from the hacked roots
of skunk cabbage—that purple, spotted thrust
to come—a sharp sour scent muscles up,
says *Live, God damn you, live!*

WAR STORY

A foot of spring snow on the ground, more incoming,
I drift off. That thunder beyond the hemlock hedge
is less the town plow than the tread of a tank.

Too much war on the brain.
Slowly, I begin to hear
what—half growl, half hum—is at the kitchen door

and rise to see
a grizzled, rat-tailed, long-nosed good-for-nothing
scavenging the cat's leftovers. I play dead

behind the glass, old bag of bones, and the possum
flexes his fur, looms large as if he's more than himself.
No, I see now, *herself*—a big-bellied undertaker

eating for a crowd of pea-sized progeny
guzzling in her fur-lined pouch. Blindly they crawled
the world of her to this nursery

in which to hide until the going's good.
I climb in myself
to wait out war—that purely human crusade.

SONG OF THE WIDOWER

All winter he did what he could for her—split firewood,
sweet apple and birch, tough locust, oak and hickory,
kept her warm by day. The fire was conversation.
But nights, when the hearth went cold
and she groaned in the silence, her windows rattling,
and settled more deeply, pipes freezing—

these were his hard times. He yearned for
in-house relations, those Dominions, to stir in the crawl
space above: blunder and whir of paper-making wasps
in March, emerged from dark cells of breathless dream,
a tapping of unfurled bats, flutter of the house wren...
And just like *that,*

it's mud time, and out from nooks in the fieldstone
cellar, garter snakes ripe with mice swell up and work
their way to the first floor, and again he shares
the pine boards of a warming kitchen with lazing
muscle boys who only half hide
in a snakeskin shaft of sun or stretch by baseboard trim.

On the middle ground of the second floor he sleeps
better—and takes in what's on its beat
in the attic, along with a *tick tick tick* created by familiars
who slept all winter with him, high up
in corners of the bedroom, dark vees of them huddled
for what little warmth they made,

who now, in the new tilt and heat of the sun, are walking
ceiling and wall, climbing window glass,
lifting the seven-spotted red of their beetle backs
to reveal they too have wings to take short flights over
puddles of light—from pane to mullion to sill,
tick, tick, tick.

It may be the sun-fire come north that incites them
but it's not, he thinks, to fly away home
that they make these puddle-jumping flights, for see
how unlady-like they are, one landing on another, quick
to make more of themselves.

Here, between such newly stirring wings on high
and such uncoiling below, risen
to the occasion, he scratches out the good news of these
inaugurations.

SWAMP SONG

This warping of the ordinary,
these weftings of song,
such trills and profundos
threading the night

unravel instantly
as ring-tailed, nimble-handed
managers of margin
fatten on the fringe and have

done
when rain begins to rattle
and raises more
stridently the ruckus of frogs.

Tomorrow the sword-beaked
Blue will hunt them
down. Their death will be
mute

as the stalk of the heron.
But now in the rain-
washed warp of the bog, such
weftings of song.

As the World Turns

He struts and pauses, turns this way and that,
the better to give her a gander at his pricked up tail,
copper-purple feathers fanned out
like a straight flush, sun-tipped and translucent.

Not looking her way, he comes closer,
his checkered side-feathers like beige fenders
hiding the mortal feet he goes upon,
bright blue head tucked close to puffed up
steel blue pectorals.
The long strand of his beard dangles orientally
below a red display of wattle.

She does not see and does not see, then carelessly
rises as if *en pointe,* stretches her wings (she has them!)
and beats the air
before she strolls obliviously into the undergrowth.

He lowers his fan, picks at mites,
then fans his tail again, pulls in his head, expands
his sun-struck, medaled chest, and meanders
toward her arch of briars.

Rock Band with Fireflies

I am too old. All the more reason to love,
from a field, flood plain and river away,
the syncopated cadence of the drums,
ground of the bass, wordless wail of rock

at the strobe-lit dance of a summer school
on its bluff across the Farmington—love
how the music comes, goes and comes again
in the currents of a cooling night,

how it matches the fireflies sparking over
the smartweed, vetch and ryegrass
of a spring-fed field and among the small
moon-struck willow leaves,

the fireflies flashing like an amplifier's
green golds, each of them a separate beat,
each signaling

I am
the one, and each one right—like the stars
in that other dance overhead, whose fires
flare up and fade and flare again.

SQUIRREL

for Sibley Watson

I am the beast, I ride the snow, my fire
burns warm within. All you with fangs,

ha! I get from here to there, I cope.
I shiver my tail for a start, and go,

leave all of my shadow behind, and stop,
wait for the shadow I threw to catch on,

then climb my tree so cleverly
I'm always on the side away from thee,

O Death with thy claws and a grin.
I win.

GETTING RELIGION

Flood's Cove, 1978

And next they're wigwamming
spruce, old pilings, driftwood,
half a lobster pot,
the rotted ladder from the pier,
topping it off with panties
and one of Debbie's bras.

Before they light her up
to show who's boss, they clown
on the roof of the lobster shed,
dive thirty feet
to water just deep enough
to prove their lives are charmed

and take to dories, work a school,
hook most of it on mackerel trees
and lay it out at the water's edge.
They hack, heave fish heads high
for gulls, leave the guts to crabs.

Now here's a sight. The boys are
silent, hunker on rockweed
to watch a thrashing of the water.
An eel is making mincemeat

of fish guts, crabs, the works.
It's five feet long, thick
as Johnny Thompson's forearm,
enough to give a boy religion.

REGATTA

All night beneath the stately turn
of the slooped and schoonered sky,
they rode the star-filled swells

expensively, their halyards chiming,
that now are under jib and spinnaker.
From this hill, this humming top,

it might be ivory queens, bishops,
kings, gowns billowing
who make their cryptic moves

across the mottled bay.
Overhead, a skein of swans,
wings working up the air to whistle,

and this for heraldry—
a blue and silver kite, an osprey,
a redtail rounding out

the sky. How hard to believe
in anything
less heavenly. But there it is,

the dive, direct hit of the hawk
and sudden tangent

to the nest,

that innerspring of rabbit rib,
shrew skin, quail down,
fox fur.

As for the yachts, the swift
white yachts,
how many among us

must be taken, bone and gut,
that these may be
so sleek?

THE DARKENING

My whirring rig makes hay,
moves in on the lively center of the field.
The dog runs circles around what goes under.

And it's done.
A low sun colors the long waves of first-cut
yellow, salmon, orange, amber

before it too goes under.
Between the darkening windrows
the meadow seems to glow from beneath

and the first fireflies, a single star, all things
which aren't going in
come out.

Walking home, I breathe easier. The dog
examines damp scents.
Now a sudden thrashing in the hedgerow

breaks into the road. And freezes.
The dog is the first to move, then the fawn,
but not fast enough—

a rent in its throat darkens. Beyond, a doe
crosses the road in a single neck-out leap.
From the other side, her shrilling

cuts through.
I have no idea how long I stand there.
In the end, the night relents,

the fireflies resume, the stars, the field.
But the rows, the long windrows
are dark as stone.

FREEZE

The dog and I are down to each other,
doing our best. She's grown her fur
thicker, my winter coat's on. We've left
the stove to see the moon

eclipsed, its silver rendered nothing
but a rusty cent. Feeling a freeze
coming on, I cover the geraniums,
tote a scuttle of coal to see us through,

lock the door, listen
to the Great Horned call the who's who
soon to be grist
and from the hill, yips rising to a howl

high-pitched and full of teeth.
The dog, all ears and nose, ruff up,
growls low in her throat. In light
of the black maw at the heart of things

I treat the dog to a bone,
stoke the stove with bits of fossil.
In the fire-door, twin eyes
of isinglass glow.

THE TRACKING

Mercury shrinks to its bulb
and the lake freezes fast
to black ice. I see myself
reflected there,

a long Walleye so slowly
passing through my head
it might be a fixed idea.
Now the stars

begin their glittering,
coy-dogs their yip and yowl.
They would have me
celebrate the Hunger Moon,

old skull in the sky.
And a cry cuts through the coys.
The lake is the white
of a wild eye.

At its heart, dark pupil,
a crippled White-tail
spins, is going nowhere.
The cry echoes from all sides.

In sudden silence, what strikes

is elegant, precise,
Manchurian. The deer is frozen,
seems to know

what the lynx
must do. One slash, she kneels;
a single lunge, her throat
is open.

Her death scream lasts
all night. In the first spill of sun
I trace the tracks
to the cache

I force myself to memorize—
ribs broken into, empty cage
of the heart, eyes staring
at me. I enter the dark

evergreens. Where the prints
are far apart, I lope,
where closer, I slow,
where closest, stop,

turn sharpened ears. At noon
I see the lynx, basking on

a boulder, oriental in the languor
of its alert. I fire in the air

and continue to fire
long after it retreats, fire
in fury,
in celebration—I have no idea.

THE TESTING

for Dean Prentis

Owl hooting. Then the scream
of a rabbit rising to the upper story
of a pine, the scream neatly
cut off.

And I am lost in badlands again,
retracing my steps in a blizzard.
Cougar prints dead center in mine
deepen abruptly and vanish

into the arc of the animal's leap
to the limb it occupies,
shoulders hunched like wings,
eyes trained on me.

And I wake to a knife at my throat,
dug in at Anzio beneath the glitter
of tracers, a cold hand on my chest
testing the bent of my dog tag,

finding me a friend. White teeth
and a whispered *Buona sera*
split the dark, then this like a flare
hissing: *The enemy, he's everywhere.*

Outside, the owl again.
How slight our cover, I think,
and turn to the give of you, my love,
the animal murmur.

BEAST IN THE ATTIC

in the Czech Republic

Today's lesson: It has rained, it is raining, it will
rain—all spring. Fat clouds hunker over
the *domecek* I've settled into.
It's time to take stock, test the attic for leaks—

this tile-roofed crawl space to which I climb,
foreign in a foreign land.
I bend low under the downpour's drubbing,
let my eyes adjust,

see something
has been here before me,
something large enough to make a gap in the wall
between the worlds. It lets in light enough to show

clumps of brown and black fur
and cairns of scat, some white, some beige or umber.
The musk has diminished: the place is mine
to sanitize.

I go down on all fours, bag in hand, ease
into my work—no hurry under this pelt of rain.
I sniff a knot of fur, cinnamon-scented, consider
the nature of the beast,

examine the various shades and curious twists
of its deposits, the earliest hollow as bird bone,
light as chalk, here for decades.
When I near its entry in a far corner,

it emerges—like a negative developing,
long and low as a stoat, ears up, aimed my way,
an ivory bib from chin to legs, a white grin
curling, sliced from the knob

at the top of my spine.
Like someone without papers
stopped at a check point, a border crossing,
I back away. I leave the attic to the animal.

THE COLLECTING

for Pablito Perras

1

First light. We cut engine, drift
to a hull just under the surface. Slow
rings pulse from it, burnished
by the early sun.

Uncle slips a hand through the noose
of the turtle line,
balances on gunwales at the bow,
launches himself,

lands flex-kneed on the Green.
Its head rears up, hissing
as he cinches the neck
and father guns the engine,
drags the turtle too many knots to dive.

I have no choice, haul it in
to my father, who flips it on its back,
slides his hand beneath the carapace
to the elbow, says she's full of eggs

and begins to club her unretracting head
methodically. Her hissing bubbles

through thickening blood
and I spit out like broken teeth
Enough, enough.

His clubbing continues, and her thudding.
Even when he carves away the under-shell,
rips out the guts
and throws them to the sharks,
the thudding of her heart continues.

Delighted, he raises it up, that delicacy.
His greatest tenderness is reserved for
the eggs he lifts out one by one.
They're worth a fortune.

2

Back in Puerto Angel, the egg-bright moon
almost full, my head against the wall
behind which my father ruts
then snores, I drift into a dark
in which I club and club his head.

Enough.
I leave, walk the silver beach,
find tracks four feet apart, away from

and back to the sea,

come on a one-way track,
against the sky a dark shape on the dune.
I crawl so close her labored breath
drowns out the surf,

wait an hour, two, until a bubble
beneath her risen stub of tail slowly
lengthens to the tube
a bulge begins its long way down.
I cup my hand below.

When it drops, that warm, I commit
the egg to memory—cream as a moon,
soft-skinned as old leather.

Already another is on its way.
I gather more than a hundred, spread them
evenly in the hole, and find myself
replacing sand,
matching her own slow swipes with mine.

It's near dawn when she turns and when,
surprising myself, I climb the carapace
I ride precariously, its sway unchanged.
My hands and feet grow raw

from gripping the rim like the edge
of a world.

In the surf I'm washed off easily, a thing
little worth remembering.

PICKEREL COVE

for David Morse

Past the local runways with their buzz of Cessnas,
beyond the last wind sock,
below a cliffside littered with junkers
rusting into the earth and pierced by saplings

curls Pickerel Cove, original coil
of the river long since gone straight, backwater home
to all the life the river's too busy to accommodate.

Find your way down, uncover the skiff,
use a snag of the stricken sycamore for balance
and put in.

There's no hurry. This will take time. You are at first
a sight for all those little periscopes
of lesser painteds peering through the scum.
Settle in, be patient, become
a part of it,

wait for the bullfrogs to begin again to claim
their pads among the pickerel weed
and the long sigh of heron wings,
the soft clap as they are folded in for the stealth
of stilt-legged fishing—signs you're safe as scenery.

It's time to move toward a disturbance

of the duckweed—a slow counterclockwise
revolution of darker algae growing
up from a two-foot shell basking
just below the surface,
from which a double-fisted, hook-beaked snout
lifts a pair of mud-black eyes to take you in.

Be still, let yourself be known. See eye to eye.
And be ready when the snapper sinks slowly,
scrapes the bottom of the boat, raises it
like the first world, setting you down, different.

Don't be surprised to feel yourself lifted up again
in deeper water at the bend,
dark, clear of algae, home to the Imperial Carp
that show themselves
just once a year when two by two they twine,
hundreds roiling the water white,
their gold-brown, black-bordered scales
the huge coins of some ancient culture.

This season you'll feel their surge well up
like the sudden updraft that catches a small plane
unawares, and tosses it,
reminder your welcome here is provisional.

THE HOLDING

It's all over. The bony maple
proves it, and the sunflowers, burnt out,
necks broken.

The tree toads think
otherwise. They gossip from limb to limb,
throats bulging ripe as melons.

And that stem-strider
exactly yellow and mold-specked enough
to make a bird think *Leaf, dead leaf*

is busy basking on a vine,
seizing the Indian day as if it's for good.
Nice way to make a living.

I can't afford it,
go on harvesting potatoes, onions, beets,
digging quickly, building up equity,

nimbly selecting the best of the crop
and heaving the rest of it
over the fence

to the lambs that browse,
oblivious to what's in store beyond
these mole-gnawed sweets.

Now it's nasturtiums, small change
I throw, rusted petals so light they float,
the frames per second fewer

and fewer. The blossoms land
on the ram, who freezes, seems to think
a single frame's enough.

Oh lord
of toads and dead-leaf bugs: for the time
being, it is. We hold our pose.

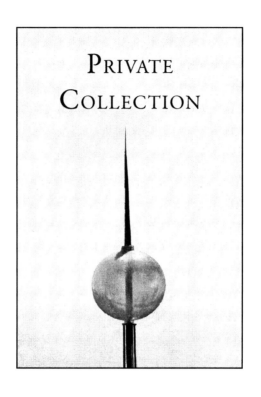

PRIVATE
COLLECTION

DIORAMA

Now you see
the diamondback's spade of a head
rear so pointedly
the frog it has in mind

poses as a lump of clay
full of hope
the snake won't know it. And now
you don't

see more than bright glass eyes,
a stretch of scales and skin
on cotton, cork and wire.

Have faith. If those two saplings
and a stone
seem unreal, they have you fooled

until halfway down a limb
or in the midst of lichen
they begin again to be pure

fabrication. Come join me here
at the seam between
the one world and the other.

IN WYETH

In Wyeth we never see
so see the more
the thunderheads
an old hound points
as if they are fair game,

and do not see
so see too vividly
in pickaxe and shovel
red with clay
at rest against a rotting stump
the old dog's death.

In Wyeth we are not shown
the way a girl who shores herself
on arms like bone
has hauled herself from house
to barn, from barn to field.
We know.

The art is to suggest, not say,
until we see
not precisely the old man's dory
scrubbed and caulked,
its bow line neatly coiled

in the bone-dry loft of a barn,

and not precisely loss
or all that makes loss gain
but something like
all three.

Last Minute

after "Sleigh Ride," Winslow Homer

Look again. There are crows
slightly darker than the sky
circling that cliff
and more below in the winterkill
around the slough.
They can barely wait.

Center left, a two-horse sleigh
on the edge of the cliff rounds a bend
too quickly. The couple within
is caught by a shaft of sun
through a rift in the sky. In no time
the dark will close on them.

But all that
will have to wait. The scene
is still on its easel, set for the painter
who enters now, biting into a windfall
Mac, his mood much improved.
He adds a dash of red,

small banner—

the lady's scarf expressing the turn
she leans into, insisting
on tea at four, a fire, festivity.
He wishes her well
against the clenching sky, the crows.

First Snow in the Garden of the Geishas

after an anonymous 18th Century Japanese print
illustrating "The Tale of Genji"

Slowly, each flake discrete, a calligraph,
the snow descends on Kyoto.
The sky is a scroll,
its characters spelling the many names
of Buddha.

In this garden of the geishas, the snow
on japonica, laurel and stone
is elaborated
by the day's last sun, like the youngest geisha
adorned for song, for dance

and pleasures more expensive.
Her face, glazed white,
is deftly rouged, kimono tied like a flower,
outlining her nape in red,
revealing the slightest hint of down.

In half an hour the paper lanterns will glow,
the plump-breasted plover on each
an invitation to the narrow lane of Pontocho.
Half an hour and the shamisen will sound,
the feast begin.

For now she walks the garden,
its pattern blurred by the bright disguise
of snow. Beneath a pretty toy bridge
glide pinioned ducks like polished
courtesans in jade and coral and ivory.

As if to bow, she bends down
to roll a seed of snow
until it is fruit, white fruit.
It grows, unveils the grounds of the garden
where half a year ago she was a novice,

drank saki from the triple cup of love,
wore on her feet the bells
to which her hair, unbound at night,
fell softly as the lavender sleeves
of her kimono.

The dark descends,
the snow fruit glows, and above it
a full-faced moon, glazed white,
leaves the world behind. Far off,
a temple bell. And the shamisen sounds.

SERVING GIRL WITH GALLANTS

after "A Woman Drinking with Two Men," Pieter de Hooch

First the checkered black and amber tiles
are bushed in, then panes of leaded glass, stage right,
allowing Delft's astonishing light to brighten
the somber room. Now it's time

to capture the tavern's newest treasure,
a slender young woman in maroon-red skirt,
tight-waisted purple tunic and linen-wimpled curls,
demure as the Virgin over the mantle. Half turned,

her small feet prim on a tile, precariously
she lifts a wine glass and through its prism sees
those slapdash gallants at table, colored quickly,
to whom she is to sing. The first taps his knee,

the other like a cricket rubs a pair of meerschaums,
winking. Judging by that red-plumed broadbrim
and orange, white-tasseled sash, they come from
the greater world of the provincial map behind them.

It's lost on them that they too are the usual
pawns, though we at one remove
see a pentimento of chessboard floor shine through
one dandy's handsome pair of oxblood boots.

Upstage, the old serving woman, eyes averted,
who brings a brazier of coals to warm the worldly
assumes her part is to be used. But the girl—
de Hooch has her hold the goblet up uncertainly

as if to shed light on on a dark passage. Her Rhenish,
kindling in a shaft of sunlight, trembles.
The painter would save her from what comes next
but is himself... If only this painting would sell.

THE RECTOR'S WIFE

for Elizabeth Rinehart McQuilkin, 1870-1938

How dark it is from the nave to the altar,
how many shades of obsidian, onyx and anthracite
in the black of his robe. And how stark
the white of his collar.

He is giving the sermon.
Behind him, her face a mask the ecru of old lace,
hands sallow as weathered bone, his wife, who once
won the conservatory's Chopin competition,

is at the organ, its keys like serried rows of
teeth. She believes in redemption,
visits the sick five days a week, calls altar flowers
a form of temptation.

For the short season of these four lines, let her be
among the roses, glads, and cosmos she was picking,
flush-faced, humming lieder,
when he came up from his other world.

after an oil by Robert Marx, title unknown

SHEEP OF PENTECOST

after "Pentecost" by Peter Ralston

At the stern of the *Edwin Drake,* surrounded
by his trawl-nets hung with block and tackle,
she has turned away from him, looks back to
the skiff in tow with its cargo

of sheep—ewes with their spring lambs
bumping teat and guzzling
in this chaos of diesel drone and mother bleat.
All those, that is, he spared from Easter slaughter.

She loves the way each lamb knows its mother
by a deep-throated call imprinted on it
in the womb—she has been singing for weeks
low down in herself.

The foam of the ocean might be the fleece
he sheered from the ewes, naked now,
being ferried to their summer grazing ground
on a barren island,

its stone cross marking the spot
where one of his forebears proclaimed *All this
is mine.* On a bluff above, she knows, is the ram,
defying capture every fall for a dozen years.

Horns sharpened on the cross,

ears aimed at the skiff, matted coat shaggy,
gold eyes cocked behind the length of its muzzle,
it waits.

In the wheelhouse he rides the sea,
has entered into a sort of pact with the ram,
she thinks—*ewes for lambs, ewes for lambs,*
the flock increasing every year.

She looks back to the diminishing steeple
in Port Clyde this day of Pentecost
and crosses her arms on the bulge
of her belly

between what she holds and a husband
who lunges in her as he pleases at night
like the prow of his trawler
bucking five-foot waves

or the ram that is said to have gored
its young and raised a 90-pound Shepherd
on its twisted horns,
tossed it from a cliff to the boulders below.

She imagines the ram caught by the coil
of its horns in a thicket of briars

and slits its upturned throat as simply as
gutting a fish.

If it wears his face, so be it. She touches
what broods in the fullness of her.

SELF-PORTRAITS

Even that docile Mannerist Christofano Allori knew—
he made the bloody head of murderous Holofernes
(held up by Judith at arm's length by a tuft of shaggy hair)
his own.

On Judgment Day in the Sistine Chapel
Michelangelo's huge executioner, skinner's knife in hand,
hoisting the trophy pelt of Saint Bartholomew
like the skin of any animal he might rest on by the fire
has the face of Michelangelo.

And Hieronymus Bosch painted himself as the centerpiece
of Hell, his torso a sort of hollow, see-through egg
full of whores and drunks. He looks back at us with such
a familiar face...

We're all in this together.
Squinting down the length of my rifle, lining up
crosshairs on the blue-black eye of an eight-foot rat snake
sliding along a white-mottled sycamore branch, homing in
on a nestful of rose-breasted fledglings,

I tighten my grip on the cold of the barrel, suspend my
breath, finger squeezing slowly, slowly,
and see the snout of the snake, framed in my sights, become
my own tight lips, the quiet, concentrated knot of my face.

ON ASSIGNMENT IN UGANDA

after a Newsweek photograph, 4/3/2000,
by Peter Andrews

I focus my lens on the boy's upper lip
with its curve and cleft of love's bow
strung with a sweet line of lower lip.

He has turned from the broken wall of
a smoldering church, has taken in what
my camera has shot—hundreds

locked inside, charred
piles of bone sparkling with shards
of stained glass. He knew them.

He holds a sprig of rosemary to
breathe through, sweeten the stench.
It doesn't

keep his lower lip from trembling,
tightening, pulling
away from the bow, beginning

to release a scream. Let it be shrill
enough to shatter the lens
I see through.

BRUEGEL'S PLAYERS

after "The Hunters in the Snow," Pieter Bruegel the Elder

How bleak these three who trudge into town
with just one fox to show for the hunt,
their lean dogs slouching behind, heads down,
man and beast dark against the sepia snow.

Above, a murder of crows waits patiently.
Only one of the houses sends up any smoke:
the people's firewood has been commandeered
for the Spanish garrison, there,

against those ice-blue cliffs. But look, oh see,
says Bruegel, the bliss
of a magpie sheering the verdigris
sky, and far below on the sky-green ice, children

skating—such tiny black ciphers enjoying
a touch of carmine for scarf, dot of pink for face.
Three of them chase a fourth; a small boy,
bent-kneed, makes a V

of his blades; another hunches down, spins a top.
To one side, hands muffed, a young woman,
thin from starvation, stops
to watch. She commits the scene to memory.

EVICTION

after an anonymous photograph, "Chicago, 1932"

I kick the door open. Like a newsreel's
flash of numbers counting down to zero
followed by the latest from the war zone,
a sudden glare

becomes a sidewalk, traffic, the el.
Small reflection in Eccle the Baker's
window, I'm wearing my Cubs cap over
a flyer's leather flaps,

also several coats, both of my holsters—
all I can take with me.
I aim one finger, thumb cocked,
at everyone staring at the odds

and ends of family—a broken loveseat,
a bureau leaking underwear,
a cracked table covered with maps
riffled by the wind—anywhere

I want to go. A boy is tugged past me
by his mother, she publicly
not looking, he backwards like an owl.
I fire and fire

and something, a mattress,
falls from a third story window,
kicks up a litter of trash—butt ends
and bits of glass.

One corner dangles in the gutter.
The ticking is filthy
with stains, some fat and tailed, some
curled like grins.

I fire at these, at the window,
the sky.
And the sidewalk opens—
old Eccle drags a sack the size of me

to the hole,
pushes it in. Scuttle of clawfeet.
The wind rattles the maps—anywhere
I want to go.

Henri Raymond Marie de Toulouse-Lautrec-Montfa

It wasn't that simple.
Besides Henri and Toulouse and Lautrec
there were those other titles to live up to
and—if you asked Rosa la Rouge
or Madame Poupoule—
some spicy sobriquets as well: Big Spout,
Corkscrew.

To begin with, then, Henri.
Communicant with certain birds and trees,
he was a child so beautiful his mother
could cry—the eyes especially, the eyes
in which his thoughts, like bright fish,
moved just below the surface.

Then Raymond—after his uncle the Count
who fell from a horse and died, humped over.
It ran in the family. For no better reason
he fell and broke himself, grew no taller
than a troll. Frog-lipped, enormously nosed,
he made a virtue of stunted legs,
declared the world to be a circus
and he its dearest freak,
a man the whores would pay to serve.

He'd rise from a night with them

and one or two hours of sleep
to gather his tools, become Marie again
devoted to his copper plates and canvases.

But he never forgot he was a Toulouse
whose people had owned the south of France
and the ear of God. He was born to it,
would tell how his mother kept a bevy of nuns
in one of her chateaus, their only duty
to pray for his sins,
which he was therefore obliged to commit.

He was, after all, Lautrec—"low tricks,"
the envious English quipped. He loved
the drunks, the can-can girls, the aging whores,
was so much a part of the brothel where
he paid handsomely for bed, board and studio
he might have been a gilded ceiling mirror.
Mornings, he stole into their rooms
to sketch the bare-faced ladies before they woke.

At the height of his notoriety, suddenly
no one, Montfa of Montparnasse no more,
he closed up shop, and suffering from lesions,
painful swelling of the testicles and penis
as well as increasing spasms of the hands and feet
and tumors in the brain inducing deafness,

went home.

Curled on the chaise longue at Malromé,
once more Henri, he asked for the songs
his mother had reserved for him,
the toy gazelle she'd saved, the silver crucifix.

An Astonishment and an Hissing

*Babylon shall become heaps, a dwelling place for dragons, an
astonishment and an hissing, without an inhabitant.*

Jeremiah, 51

And it was as the hand had written on her wall:
the Jewel of the East, Lady of Two Rivers,
Ark of Ishtar and Marduk—Babylon

was dust. The wonder of her gardens hung to veil
too fragrant communion from the jealous gods,
her Tower of Towers,

the manacled dragons inlaid along her avenues
and sculpted kings brazen as the bulging sun
that crouched behind the Tigris,

her myriad victories
carved in ivory set in lapis lazuli—all
were broken, all burned.

After the pitch that bound her bricks
ran boiling in the streets, and golden gods, gone
molten, flowed in channels carved for blood,

after the perfumed cedar of ceilings cooled to ash
and even Alexander, kicking through the rubble,
grew weak at the thought of raising her again—

after her shame was all the world could wish,
Jehovah wished more, uncoiled long muscles,
and sinuous as script, slid into her, hissing.

In the end, the brown-voiced Euphrates
and wailing siroccos
buried her under centuries of silt and sand,

buried all but the ghost of Nebuchadnezzar.
Ox-bodied, buzzard-clawed, he crawls
the desert over Babylon.

GETAWAY

after an early work by Mack Burns, age 3

He crayoned his first crèche in three parts.
All's well at the top—the Firmament is
heavenly blue. But the Sky
is trouble. It's full of what—stars or angels
swarming like a plague of leggy spiders.

Just above the manger is a star burst
from something like a Scud
incoming. Part Three has the Baby Jesus
the size of his parents, his feet and head
protruding from a purple perambulator.

A lush brown, black-haired Mary,
her arms and one leg colored jaggedly,
leans forward as if to wheel the giant baby,
hissing to the blueblood blob of Joseph
"Let's get out of here!"

The space around the shed is fire-orange
except for a—camel? Brown as Mary
and humped high as the ridgepole,
it's kicking a hole in the siding. To knock
sense into Joseph's head? Or show it's

raring to go? Maybe left by a Wise Man

after he informed on the king. But—
shouldn't it be a donkey? A minor mistake.
Thank God for its headstrong headful
of a stall somewhere Herod never heard of.

St. Gregory of the Golden Mouth

*Born on Inis Mór in the Aran Islands, sent to Rome in 398. His
coffin is said to have floated to his birthplace in Cill Rónáin. Not
recognized by Rome. He is the subject of a stained glass window
in the small chapel near Synge's Seat on the island of Inis Meáin.*

I was so pretty a pagan the Abbot said he'd have
me sent to Rome—it was a sin the way I cavorted
from crag to crag in uncured sandals
with the fur still bristling on their soles.

I let myself be sent, hating as I did
the stench of burning dung
that hovered like the Aran fog in small stone rooms
and the beat of the terrible rock-breaking waves

on which the brittle black currachs were tossed
like upended beetles, all six oars flailing.
My own father was taken by the breakers
at Bungowla, dashed against the rocks and flayed,

brought home in pieces and puzzled together
by three crones keening like the wind
and warning me to kiss his frozen lips or be going
straight to hell.

His father's bones,
bits of gristle clinging, were dug from their patch

of dirt—old poverty of clay and crumbled stone—
for him to be planted in their place

and soon uprooted for the likes of me. I traded that
for the elegance of Rome, where my golden words
elevated me at the Vatican, the Celtic savage
civilized by velvet robes, at home

with the finest the City could offer,
drinking in the sweet marrow of its osso buco
washed down with papal wine. My new ways came
easily. Something lost must have risen in me

the way sweet-water on the Islands,
siphoned off by limestone swallow holes
to carve out underworlds, would—*mirabile dictu*—
reappear. This lasted thirty years.

I was not prepared, in the midst of Matins,
for the welling up
of Inis Mór's cursive loop-holed walls
the early sun shone through, embellishing,

wives at ease on the beach at Cill Mhuirbhigh,
circled in mauve or red by their rings of skirt,
and a stone-gray pony backlit on a crag
above Dún Eochla, mane cresting like the surf.

Serving Mass this morning, I saw an open coffin
lengthen to a currach
bearing my gray and glittering remains
to three islands brightly green on a burgundy sea.

for Gray Jacobik, who introduced me to St. Gregory

DESERT

Humpbacked with gear, my water
exhausted, I stumble on a mule deer,
eyes lively with maggots.

The buzzards are all
but done. Clack of beak on beak,
a sharpening. The sand burns,
rises about me like the aura of flies
about the deer.

Around another bend, another,
and there in a recess
low on the canyon wall
rust, white and ochre dancers,
torsos tapering like arrowheads.

Their heads are skulls,
eyes enormous,
robes ornamented with antelope.
Birds occupy their shoulders.
Beside them, snake spirits rise like
walking sticks.

A dust devil spins where I stand
at the foot of the talus
and settles. The heat returns,

the canyon walls resume
their wavering, and the dancers
repeat their deliberate step.

The drumming of distant thunder
is merely the thrum of a hummingbird
hovering by snakeweed.
I find an alcove in which to begin
to be bone, picked clean—

and wake to wet wind, the scent
of creosote bush, tall clouds rising
over the rimrock, dark as flint.
Lightning flickers, the rain begins.

LADDERS TO GLORY

The drawbridge grinds its gears,
leans on the sky, a kind of ladder.
Its rungs—well, see for yourself
how well versed those I-beams are

in row on row of—not smut
but what anyone with a ten-inch
brush and gallon of Glidden would
inscribe at high tide on the bottom

of a thing that low that ready to
expose itself: Day Glo billets doux
in script a full foot tall. SC DOES
IT, I'm glad to hear. But just now
I'm boating into open water.

And look—through the cumulus
a ladder of light is being lowered,
gulls ascending and descending.
Glad you feel that way up there.
I'll do my best.

GOING UNDER

for my mother and father

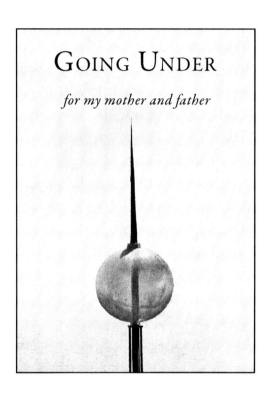

BLACK ICE

First ice on the lake.
Sounds carry like skipping-stones:
the squeak of distant skates,
tags on a dog by the opposite shore.

Through ice so clear
it's the color of lake, I see what
summer obscured:
trout, all facing one way.

Somewhere below, dug into mud,
a thing in a shell like any continent
is dreaming up another spring.

And you, father, have grow so other-
worldly, the skin of your present
so transparent

you allow us to see
clean through to the kingdom
of your childhood—it holds

against the current.
And deeper down in you is what
knows a stone can skip forever

if it's flat enough
and the wrist is cocked just so—

what knows a death
is the skip that keeps us going.

Rescue

Driving home to pull my father out
of his oblivion, I go off the road,
carom steeply,
miss an abutment by inches.

While a wrecker digs in and pulls
I hear I'm a lucky guy.
I know, but not just yet. Give me time.
All the way to Dox's Garage, Dox doesn't.

Could be worse, he says, and shows me
a Dodge full of glass,
the soggy char of seats, the remains
of a shoe. Some body work's all I need,

he says. The red sun, sinking, means
delight, says Henry,
who comes for me, full of society. I see
only an abutment.

Home, my father has no idea
who I am. What he's staring at is
beyond me. I have nothing
to say, just hold him and hold him.

GOING UNDER

He no longer cares
for himself. I undress him,
strip down, lead him into
this sort of confessional,

adjust the spray.
Marble legs, blue veined,
amethyst penis too small,
brown coral on his back.

Clearly not my father,
something from the bottom
discovered by a boy
diving for drachmas.
I won't have it.

I lather him, scrub his back,
then more gently
his buttocks, between his legs,
the calves, the shins.

With a grinding of bone
on bone, he lifts an arm,
begins his song. I understand
nothing, not a word I sing,
repeating after him.

COMPANY

He squints at me.
—*What company are you with, young man?*
—*I'm not, daddy, I'm writing a book,*
I'm my own company.
—*Yes, of course, I have a son does that.*

When I try to lead him from the corner
where he has propped himself, he digs in,
has forgotten how to walk.

In the hall my brother smiles sadly
from his other world of T'ai Chi,
wheeling an arm as if something wants up
through the soles of his feet.

I work my father's arms like an old
nutcracker's, and he raises
first one foot then the other onto mine.
I count cadence and *hay foot, straw foot*
march him counterclockwise.

Go to your left your right your left
past Michael's windmill, *Left o-blique*
at the living room, and he's on his own
two feet, and lord how we *Sound off 1-2,*
sound off 3-4, harmonizing:

I got a girl lives on a hill
Says she won't, but I know she will.

The china rattles, the glassware chimes.
And Michael's arm goes
round and round. Whoever he is,
whoever I am, whoever this man saluting
left and right,
we are for now a company.

Birthday at the Motor Vehicle Dept.

In line to be renewed
I inch toward the counter,
deep in my separate dark.
At intervals, a flash.

I am called up, hand over
my self,
sit for a new one, become
this small card,

surprisingly warm.
The face is beyond me,
distorted as if under water,
and surfaces—

my father's, propped up
by pillows
to keep him from drowning.
His breath slogs,

stops.
And slogs again.
I dampen his cracked mouth,
change the compress

on his brow, take the heat.

He tries to clear the death
from his throat. It rises.
His eyes go higher than I

can follow,
his colors fade to beige,
then ivory.
I smooth out his face,

trace his softened lips,
his nose, unflared,
and cover his eyes.
His warmth has passed

to me, old relay. I'm left
with this license—my name,
birthdate, and the red
pronouncement: *Donor.*

YOUR THINGS

I'm feeling small, father,
going through things you won't be needing
like these jade and ivory kings and bishops
you played to win

and did, the way you always won, even
as a kid. No one's baseball cards stood up
to the Cobbs and Goslins you pitched
at their heads.

And here, a bag of marbles.
Your aggies went ba bam, didn't they?
I know. Whenever I missed a trick
your eyes would roll at me, dead on,

knock me out of the game.
For days you'd carry me in your pocket,
polishing.
Next time I'd be sure-fire.

I'll never shake you. Your smell
is in these three-piece herringbones
and size thirteens
I tried to clown in, hating the smell,
the press of it,

like the closet full of you

I hid in, hating
how you gripped my hand to make a boy
a man, how you hugged the air from me. I—

Father, I'd risk my finger bones, my ribs,
and all the rest
if the pile of coats and pants I hold
like you
would have a go at me.

DISCOVERY

on going through my mother's papers

In a photo of my parents courting, spring break at Oxford,
the sun illuminates my handsome father, casts the bulk of
his shadow on my mother, who all but
disappears. Which is how it was when I came into the picture.

Only years later, after he went under, did she emerge.
And even then I didn't know her full worth, couldn't see
until—how shall I put this? Perhaps you've heard
about the Villa of the Lost Papyri in Herculaneum, buried

by Vesuvius: those fountains, arcades, mosaics, stunning
hall of marble nudes, obsidian busts with jade and ivory eyes.
When archaeologists unearthed such treasure
and descended into dark archives to look for more,

they puzzled over hundreds of cylinders dark as coal,
burned some against the cold, kept hunting
until one day someone noticed characters inscribed
on the cylinders. As these were slowly unraveled, they saw

papyrus nearly destroyed but in the end preserved by
disaster, a trove of lost philosophy, drama, poetry—
words for which, without their knowledge, they'd waited
as I, dear mother, have waited unknowingly for yours.

INVITATION

Mother has shown me the secret
bowl of twigs and twine,
snake skin, horse hair and rabbit fur
in forsythia
trimmed like a hood.

From here, waxwings,
expecting, sang all April
their yellow, tawny, crested songs.
They were mistaken.
They left.

She's careful to leave a gap
in the forsythia for their return
and in herself another
for whoever she was when she was
at home in herself, a schoolgirl

skating, polka dotted clown suit
billowing, huge ruffles at the neck,
one leg in the air like a tail,
arms out for balance, head cocked
to sing.

COMET-WATCHING
IN THE PITTSFORD CEMETERY

Easter Sunday, 1997

Meal worms have had a field day
in her spices and cereals. When I find
the winged things they've become
are too quick to catch, she's not surprised.

They're angels, she quips, and may half
believe, so many loves have gone under.
Her world's increasingly peopled
with them. Today she planted a totem

blackbird, beak upright with song,
by her husband's tall stone which doubles
as her own, just one of the four dates
still open. At dusk she leads me there—

hill city glowing under a waxing moon—
to see the brightest comet of the century,
twin-tailed and lucid as a Luna,
powder the sky with the stuff we are of.

COASTING

Still hale if frailer
at year's end, housebound
for your eighty-eighth
solstice, two feet of snow

already down,
the house lights flickering,
you laugh to see
through double panes

what rides out the blizzard—
an oak leaf,
brown, sere, curled edges up,
coasting the crust.

Get Used to Endings

she says, undone by another,
shuffling down the dust-
hung lane past the old scrub oaks.

She goes slowly,
stops often for breath, too much
a part of this décor

to worry a towhee rustling up grubs
or an osprey on a roadside pole
webbing a wattled nest with fishnet.

She commits it all
to memory, happy to be here to see
again a black swan whistling over

so low she's stirred by the wind
of its wings. Three beats, it's gone.
And she goes on.

THE LIGHTERS

In her eighty-ninth year she's reducing
her inventory—china to the children, mementos
to the trash—but in her boudoir
keeps half a dozen square-shouldered Zippos,

on one her husband's initials,
the best man's on another, the rest anyone's guess.
Dry-chambered, their rusted spark wheels stalled,
they are lined up gravely on a jewelry chest

full of antique gap-toothed keys with elaborate
scrollwork on their hilts, fit to open
high-backed steamer trunks, perhaps the door
to a sunken garden

where every night the dry-bones come
in mothballed flannels and hand-knit sweaters
to roll their own, light up
like fireflies and, sotto voce, remember her.

LUMINATION

The stories my mother and I tell
on each other at this festival of light
are only harmless

to others at the table.
Now she leans unsteadily to
blow out candles held by clay angels

and her fine white hair catches fire.
It blazes, illuminating the terrified
naughts of her eyes and mouth.

Later, still smelling burnt hair
on these hands that put out the fire
with a fierce laying on,

I think how soon her hair
will again be the first of her
to burn, this time beyond my reach.

I've lost
interest in the stories I tell.
My hands know better.

THE CANE

Knotty, brass-collared, its bone handle
grooved like wrinkled skin,
the eye of a heron at its crook,
her father's cane went everywhere
with her. When airport security
suspected its hickory
hid contraband,
she shook it, feigned senility,
prevailed.
The less she trusted her pins
the more she trusted the cane to keep her
from a walker or, God help her, wheels.
With it she strode the fairway
of her kitchen, hip-
swinging like her favorite linkster,
and when she took to bed for
good, she kept it close,
would need its support on her journey,
kissed its ivory beak, got a grip on it below
the covers, and when she let go at last,
would not let go of it.

MORNING NEWS

This ritual: a clean-out
of the firebox, a plume of ash
rising like an empty speech balloon,

the twisting of yesterday's news
to kindling, a laying on of
thin-split birch,

the opening of windows—a jolt
of weather without which the fire
will die, which catches now.

In the dark before dawn, I love
the crackling woodstove's gossip,
shades of your good

morning news, my dear. If only
I could have let in more air
when your breath began to fail

and snapped my fingers like striking
a match to make you leap up—
sure fire, my day's first flame.

FLY-OVER

I don't know what the black swans do
or where they go, only know how they pass,
how I hear them far off, coming in low
over the dunes, no noisy honking like geese

but a whip-whistling
of wings, not slow like herons' but *quick,
quick*... and there they are,

working the ocean air like dolphins, undulating
the long muscles of serpentine neck and
ebony fuselage, the water-raking feet pulled in,
heading back at dusk through the low red sun.

There, mother, I've made the swans the way
you liked them, and now I'm waiting for them
as you waited before you too went where
I don't know.

Just a year ago today we were
together here, where I watch as if in a blind.
And—*quick, quick*—they're coming, but only
one—and that one white. White. And gone.

LORD GOD BIRD

When I heard the news, mother, I wanted to
call to make it real, hear you yelp
when I told you *The Lord God Bird is back,*
no longer extinct, forgetting, as ever, that you are.
Extinct, that is.

I'm always brought up short by the news.
How? There was so much of you—like the Ivory Billed
that wouldn't let Death get away with a thing,
tore the rotting bark off stricken trees
with that box-cutter beak, eating its weight in beetles.

And there it is, they say, still
sounding off like a factory whistle—*Work, work,*
the day has come—still excavating caves in deadwood,
still flashing red, white and black
through the gloom of old-growth bogs.

And you, mother,
oh Lord God how you come and go in the dismal dark!

NOTES

Page 55, "End of the Season": Snapping Turtles, which reach prodigious sizes and ages, are surprisingly affable in the water (though not on land, where they are vulnerable). When they take their siestas, lying just under the surface, they will allow a slow-boater to sidle up and scratch their shells with a paddle. Perhaps they like the scraping of algae.

Page 87, "The Hole": Lava Falls is the most nororious of the rapids in the stretch of the Colorado that flows through the Grand Canyon. Getting caught in the "hole" at the heart of Lava Falls has been fatal for many river-runners. On the occasion described here, the hole was especially unpredictable and dangerous because of high waters.

Page 89, "Last": Every fourteen days another language dies out.

Page 110, "After Waterloo, What": Many historians believe that Napoleon was murdered by his wine steward, who was in league with the British general charged with preventing Napoleon's escape from the desert island of St. Helena. The speculation is that over a period of time enough arsenic was added to Napoleon's wine to cause a death whose origin could not be detected. The evidence includes an extraordinary amount of arsenic in hair samples taken from Napoleon, as well as his bloated condition during the weeks before his death and the surprising lack of bodily decay found when he was exhumed for burial in France, which has been attributed to the preservative property of arsenic.

Page 132, "Valentine": James Merrill was fascinated by the voices that spoke through the movement of a planchette on his ouija board.

Page 157, "The Tracking": Large cats (lions, leopards and even lynx) are able to project their voices so that they seem to be on all sides of their prey.

Page 160, "The Testing": During World War Two, special units were detailed to kill Germans posing as Allied infantry. Members of those units would leap into foxholes at night and slit the throats of any whose dog tags had the smoothly elliptical shape of the German type.

Page 162, "Beast in the Attic": The beast was, in fact, a pine marten, a member of the weasel family even more ferocious than the notorious North American Fisher.

Page 164, "The Collecting": Sea turtles are unable to retract their heads, which makes it possible to rope their necks.

Page 180, "First Snow in the Garden of the Geishas": The traditional indoctrination of geishas was demanding and their initiation highly ceremonial (less so nowadays when geishas are pale imitations of their predecessors). They were expected to master not only the art of love but also the arts of dance, theater, poetry and music. The instrument most often played by geishas has always been the shamisen, a long-necked stringed instrument resembling a banjo (in shape only).

Page 185, "Sheep of Pentecost": In the Christian calendar, Pentecost, occurring on the fiftieth day after Easter, marks the occasion when the Apostles, being filled with "tongues of fire," were able to speak the truth prophetically.

Page 190, "Bruegel's Players": References to the Spanish fortress, commandeering of firewood, and starvation derive from the occupation of the Lowlands by Hapsburg forces at the time when Pieter Bruegel the Elder was active as a painter. Many of his works were protests against the occupation (e.g., "The Massacre of the Innocents," in which Herod's soldiers, sent to slay all male children of two years or less, are clearly Hapsburg cavalry). Even the Lowland spelling of Bruegel's name, from which he dropped the "h," was an act of defiance.

Page 193, "Henri Raymond Marie de Toulouse Lautrec-Montfa": As a boy, Toulouse Lautrec broke both of his thigh bones, and because of a genetic disorder, his legs failed to grow, leaving him dwarfed, though his torso and head were normal. It is said that he had hypertrophied genitals.

Page 196, "An Astonishment and an Hissing": It is interesting to note the similarity between Babylon and Baghdad. The ancient city (adjacent to Sadam Hussein's palace) was located close to present-day Baghdad, though any resemblance between George Bush and Jehovah, the Destroyer of Babylon, is purely coincidental.

Page 203, "Desert": The narrator probably refers to pre-Anasazi pictographs lining 150 feet of a shallow alcove in what is now called Horseshoe Canyon, a part of Canyonlands National Park in Utah. The site is known as the Grand Gallery; it is the lengthiest series of pictographs yet discovered.

Page 217, "Your Things": The game of marbles referred to is the one that is played "for keeps": that is, winning players get to keep the marbles of the losers, who have then lost their marbles.

INDEX OF POEMS

About the Author

Rennie McQuilkin's work has appeared in *The Atlantic, Poetry, The Southern Review, The Yale Review, The Hudson Review, The American Scholar, The Gettysburg Review, Chelsea, Crazyhorse, Prairie Schooner*, and elsewhere. This is his tenth poetry collection. McQuilkin has received numerous awards for his work, as well as fellowships from the National Endowment for the Arts and the State of Connecticut. For many years he directed the Sunken Garden Poetry Festival, which he co-founded at Hill-Stead Museum in Farmington, Connecticut. In 2003 he received a Lifetime Achievement Award from the Connecticut Center for the Book. With his wife, the artist Sarah McQuilkin, he lives in Simsbury, CT, where he is the local poet laureate and publishes poetry by Northeastern authors.

COLOPHON

THE WEATHERING is set in Garamond Premier Pro, which had its genesis in 1988 when type-designer Robert Slimbach visited the Plantin-Moretus Museum in Antwerp, Belgium, to study its collection of Claude Garamond's metal punches and typefaces. In the mid-1500's Garamond, a Parisian punch-cutter, produced a refined array of book types that combined an unprecedented degree of balance and elegance, for centuries standing as the pinnacle of beauty and practicality in type-founding. Slimbach has created a new interpretation based on Garamond's designs and on comparable italics cut by Robert Granjon, Garamond's contemporary. The front cover of *The Weathering* is set in Mayflower, a typeface used for the Geneva Bible of 1610, which was preferred by English Protestants and carried to America by the Pilgrims.

To order additional copies of *The Weathering*
or other Antrim House titles, contact the publisher at

Antrim House
P.O. Box 111, Tariffville, CT 06081
860.217.0023, AntrimHouse@comcast.net
or the house website (www.AntrimHouseBooks.com).

•

On the house website are
sample poems, upcoming events, and a
"seminar room" with supplemental biography,
notes, images and poems, as well as discussion topics
and writing suggestions offered by Antrim House authors.